The Gun Digest Book of

Gun Care Cleaning & Refinishing

Book Two: Long Guns

by J. B. Wood

DBI Books, Inc., Northfield, Ill.

About Our Covers

In case you hadn't noticed, the "Good Old Boys" at Omark/CCI added Outers Labs to their growing family of products for shooters.

As we all know, Outers has a long-standing, superb reputation with shooters and hunters worldwide. We are indeed proud to have Outers' products featured on the outside cover of this the *Gun Digest Book of Gun Care, Cleaning & Refinishing, Book Two: Long Guns*.

In the center of the cover you'll see one of Outers latest offerings. It's their new Silverline rifle case, made of tough aluminum and featuring egg-carton type foam lining for maximum firearms protection; the case is, of course, lockable for security.

Surrounding the new Silverline case is a selection of Outers gun care and maintenance products. They include an Outers Stock Finish Kit, the new "Imperial" line of top quality one-piece cleaning rods, a standard Outers 3-piece cleaning rod and the new Imperial Shotgun Chamber & Gas Port cleaning rod. Also seen is a sampling of Outers new line of aerosol gun cleaning products. To the left is a can of Outers Crud Cutter™, a degreaser, and to the right a can of Outers Nitro Solvent bore cleaner.

Our Inside Covers feature one of the oldest gun-care equipment outfits in the the U.S., RIG Products Company. For almost a half-century RIG has provided shooters with their famous Rust Inhibiting Grease ("RIG Universal"). It's designed to fully protect a firearm from the elements of foul weather, or serve as long term protection during storage.

On our inside front cover you'll see a jar and tube of the traditional RIG Universal grease as well as a jar each of RIG +P Stainless Steel Lube and RIG Black Powder Patch Lube. Also present is an aerosol can of RIG 3, a superb degreaser, and an aerosol can of RIG 2 Oil Lubricant.

In the center are some of RIG's newest offerings. They include a bronze action brush, a RIG-Rod for rifles, along with bronze brushes and loop-tips in various calibers. The bronze action brush as well as the RIG-Rod and accessories are all resting on the traditional sheepskin RIG-Rag.

Seen on our inside back cover is, of course, a jar of RIG Universal grease, followed by some of the newer members of the RIG family of gun-care products, including: RIG 3, a superb degreaser, RIG 2, a light-oil lubricant and a jar of RIG +P Stainless Steel Lube (a sample of which is included with every Randall Stainless Steel auto that leaves the factory).

Also pictured: a tube of Universal grease, a sheepskin RIG-Rag and the new, custom-quality RIG-Rod for handguns, complete with jags, brushes and loop tips. Photos by John Hanusin.

ISBN 0-910676-82-8

About the Author

Guns, especially automatic pistols, have always been a part of J.B. Wood's life, and it has now been almost 35 years since he began working as a gunsmith. Fortunately, Wood has been able to combine his mechanical talents with writing about them, which he's been doing since 1962. In that time he has had more than 400 articles published in *Gun Digest, Guns Illustrated* and in most of the monthly gun magazines. In 1977-78 he authored a two-book series for DBI Books, *Troubleshooting Your Handgun* and *Troubleshooting Your Rifle and Shotgun*. From 1979 to 1981, Wood wrote and photographed the six-part *Firearms Assembly/Disassembly* series, a monumental task that turned out to be the best reference ever printed on the subject at hand.

In 1974, J.B. Wood began a regular monthly relationship with the gun magazines. He was Gunsmithing Editor for *Guns & Ammo* magazine for eight years, is Contributing Editor to *Gun Digest* and *Combat Handguns*, and currently is Gunsmithing Editor for *Shooting Times* magazine. Because he is so well briefed on firearms in general, and self-loading pistols in particluar, Wood is considered to be an international authority, and has testified in many court cases involving firearms as an expert witness. In addition, he has done mechanical design and redesign work for a number of domestic and foreign arms makers. Currently he is a full-time gunsmith, writer, and firearms consultant and lives in rural Kentucky.

Arms and Armour Press, London, G.B., exclusive licencees and distributors in Britain and Europe; Australaiasia, Nigeria, South Africa and Zimbabwe; India and Pakistan; Singapore, Hong Kong and Japan.

Library of Congress Catalog Card #84-071764

Table of Contents

Acknowledgements

My thanks to these people, who helped to make this book possible:

Doug Wright, Charles Magee, Arnold Carlson, Al Selleck, Lee Keppler, Bill Cooper, Bob and Frank Brownell, Ted Bottomley, Jim Brobst, Doug Evans, Brady Brown, Richard Simons, John Stupero, Anthony Rupp, Ted Freeland, Bill Wilson, Jim Kelley, Alexander Zemke, Richard Floyd, Darrell Reed, Foxi Maguire, Ronnie Butler, Al Paulsen, Pauline McIntosh, Jim and John Yarger, Frank Droege, Spike Brown, Robert Greenberg, Milton Settar, Robert Ellsworth, Michael Kera, Dale Davis, and Wayne Gurowsky.

A special thanks to Michael Schmidt, for his expert developing and printing of my photos.

Introduction

OVER THE PAST 10 years, in my magazine column, "The Gunsmith", I've handled a lot of firearms questions. In every packet of letters from readers, there are certain questions that I know will be there. They'll want to know how much a gun is worth, or where to find a particular part, or how to disassemble and reassemble their guns. The value questions I usually side-step, because no really valid figure can be set without an actual examination of the piece. Sometimes, for a good general estimate, I recommend two fine DBI books, *Modern Gun Values,* and Flayderman's monumental book covering antique American guns.

For the parts questions, I can usually give a known source for new or used replacements. I have an easy answer for the takedown and reassembly inquiries—most of them are referred to the six-volume set of books on this subject produced by this writer and DBI Books.

Some questions, though, can't really be covered well in the one-paragraph space of a monthly column. Here's an example: Is it harmful to leave the magazine of a repeating rifle or shotgun fully loaded for a long period of time? Will it weaken the magazine spring? This question could be put under the general heading of "Gun Care."

Another example is this one, and it would require a more extensive answer: Many experts say that the direction of cleaning should always be from the chamber to the muzzle, especially in rifled barrels. However, quite a few rifles and shotguns can't be cleaned that way. Will cleaning from the muzzle end harm the rifling? This is not the sort of question that can be properly handled in a quick one-paragraph answer, because there are too many factors involved. The category for this one would obviously be "Cleaning."

Questions about refinishing are another regular occurrence. Gun people want to know what type of finish to choose, and whether refinishing will lower the value of certain guns. A few years ago I wrote two articles for *Guns Illustrated* that covered the finishes that were available at that time. Several new finishes have been introduced since then, and many gun people know them only by name. With the three questions mentioned above in mind, this writer and DBI Books decided to give a thorough treatment to these subjects—**Care, Cleaning,** and **Refinishing.** One-half of the result is the book you are now reading (the other volume covers handguns).

It should be noted that the Refinishing section of this book is definitely *not* a how-to-do-it guide. It's a description and evaluation of the currently-offered finishes, to help the reader in making a wise choice.

J. B. Wood
Raintree House
Corydon, Kentucky

Section One

Gun Care

I'VE BEEN A gunsmith for a long time, and when someone mentions the proper "care" of rifles and shotguns, the first thing that comes to my mind is the mechanical aspect—dry-firing, leaving the magazine loaded for long periods of time, and so on. Care, though, should cover a lot more than just the mechanical questions. It should also include handling safety, proper storage, security from theft, and other things. In writing about some of these, I'll inevitably cover some points that are well known to experienced hunters and shooters. It may be, though, that some who will be reading this book will be beginners. So, for them, I'll try to cover even the elementary things.

Mechanical questions are still the most important, so I'll start with one of the most frequent inquiries: Is it harmful to "snap" a rifle or shotgun when it's empty? There is no quick and simple answer to this one. With the exception of the lever-action rifles, most modern repeating rifles and shotguns do not have an external hammer that can be let down easy. So, when the gun is put away after a day of shooting, it is often a practice to pull the trigger and drop the internal hammer or striker, to ease the tension on the spring. (More about this factor, a little further on). Many shooters and hunters will tell you that this dry firing has never harmed their guns. There are, though, quite a few cases in which firing pin breakage and other damage can be directly attributed to dry firing. Some guns are more tolerant of this than others, so this factor often depends on the design of the particular gun.

Let's look at the mechanical effect of dry firing on the firing pin: When there is a cartridge in the chamber, the firing pin point has its impact sort of softened as it strikes the relatively soft metal of the primer. This is the principle used in the "snap caps" often used with fine shotguns. Those consist of a dummy shell that has the primer replaced with a plug of resilient material to cushion the impact of the firing pin. Brownells, the famed gunsmith supply firm, (Route Two, Box One, Montezuma, Iowa

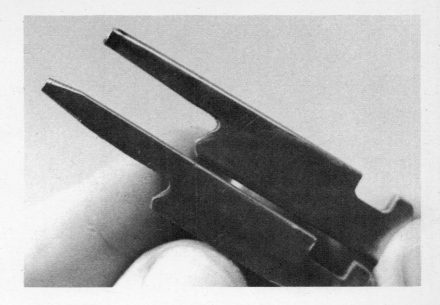

These two firing pins, from slide action shotguns, both have broken points. The one above shows an attempted repair by brazing, an operation that is usually unsuccessful. It is probable that the broken tips were caused by dry-firing.

Offset 22 rifle firing pins such as these are prone to dry-firing breakage. The tool indicates the location of the broken point.

50171) has economical snap-caps in 12, 20, 28, and 410 gauge, and they cost around $6 each. Each has a neoprene ring to keep it in the chamber, and a spring-powered nylon "primer." The body is solid aluminum alloy.

Getting back to the effect of dry firing, when the chamber is empty, the firing pin is stopped very suddenly and abruptly. A metallurgist once described the effect for me, and if my terminology is a little off, the errors are mine: If a very small piece of steel (a firing pin point, for example) is in motion and is stopped suddenly, some of the molecules in the steel continue to drift in the original direction of movement. Repeating this action will increase the density of the point, until it becomes brittle. This process is, I suppose, a form of metal fatigue.

When the firing pin is given an extra-hard tempering at the factory, this process will be speeded up. I have seen numerous examples of

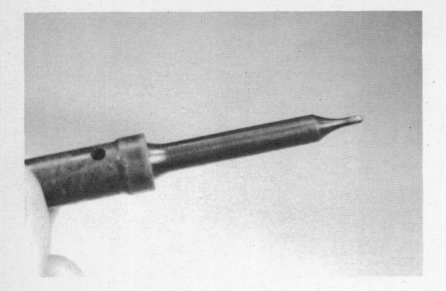

An ideal firing pin shape is illustrated by the point of this striker from a Japanese Arisaka rifle. The sweeping line from the body of the pin to the point makes it less likely to fracture.

These Pacific Snap-Caps, available from Brownells, are made of solid aluminum. They have a nylon "primer" with a spring cushion, and a neoprene ring to keep the unit in the chamber. They are inexpensive, and, for internal-hammer shotguns, an excellent idea.

this, and after the crystallization break, the remaining point is often so hard it can be used to mark glass. When making replacement firing pins in my shop, I always use semi-hardened drill rod, and I give it no heat-treatment at all. Firing pins that I have made in this manner for my own guns are still in use, after many years.

Two other important factors are the mass of the firing pin, and the distance it moves. For example, the effect is not as pronounced with the small, short firing pins of a modern double shotgun. In guns that have long, slim firing pins, breakage tends to be more frequent. Also, the long but heavy strikers of target rifles, which have a very short fall for more rapid lock-time, rarely break.

Some have expressed the opinion that in guns that have a strong firing pin return spring and a separate hammer, the spring will have a cushioning effect on the firing pin, in the same way

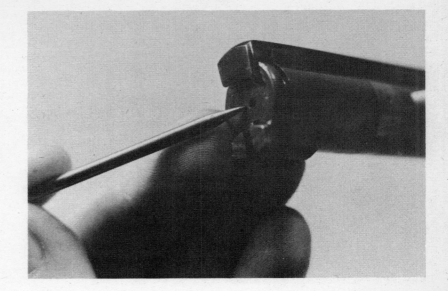

In centerfire rifles, the bolt face will have enough thickness to preclude any deformation of the aperture from dry-firing.

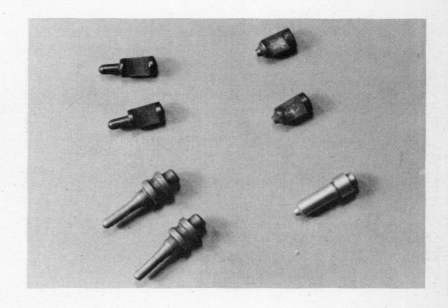

The firing pins of single-barrel and double-barrel shotguns. Breakage is usually from over-hardening rather than from impact stress. These short pins lack the mass that contributes to impact embrittlement.

as the snap-caps mentioned earlier. In some specific cases, this may have some validity, but in most guns, the amount of mass involved and the degree of spring tension will tend to cancel each other, so this should not be generally depended upon.

When the gun in question is a 22 rimfire, dry firing is always a thing to be avoided. There are a few guns which have firing pins designed to stop before the point reaches the rear face of the barrel, but most are not in this category. Even guns designed with this feature may eventually have more protrusion as the shoulder of the firing pin or its stop in the tunnel is peened or eroded. In any 22, it's best to just assume that the firing pin point will touch the barrel. When the point hits the barrel at the edge of the chamber, it will begin to dent it. When this becomes severe, it can interfere with loading and extraction. By this time, there will usually be break-

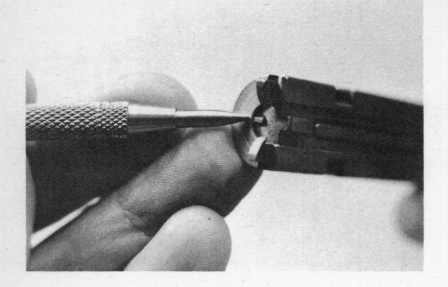

In this fine Krico 22 rifle, the firing pin point has exactly the right protrusion, and would not impact on the rear face of the barrel if the chamber were empty. Many rimfire guns, though, are not so carefully engineered.

Most double shotguns have fairly thin breech face walls at the firing pin aperture, and excessive dry-firing can cause an extrusion of the steel around the aperture. In the gun shown, this has not occurred.

age of the firing pin point.

A few of the serious 22 target pistols have a dry-firing device as part of the design, a lever that can be engaged (with the hammer at rest) to simulate trigger pull for practice. There may be a similar provision on some 22 target rifles, but if so, I haven't seen one. Generally, the best rule to follow with any 22 rimfire rifle is to avoid snapping it when empty. Most now have hammers or strikers powered by coil springs, so

there's no harm in leaving them cocked.

There is another type of damage that can occur from dry-firing, and I've noticed it especially in double shotguns that have very short firing pins. The impact of the shoulder behind the firing pin point on the inner ledge of the firing pin tunnel can upset the breech face at the firing pin hole. When this is excessive, it can cause the shell heads to bind. In one severe case that I know of, it caused the gun to fire when

The Ithaca Model 66 is no longer made, but there are still a few shotguns with alloy receivers. In these, dry-firing should particularly be avoided.

closed! This can occur in any gun in which the point of the firing pin is relatively short and the breech face is not thick. Firing pins are normally harder than the breech face of any gun, so this is a factor to be considered.

Some low-priced shotguns of recent manufacture have receivers made of zinc or aluminum alloys, and this can contribute to yet another area of dry-firing damage. In guns of this type, the steel hammer impacts on the rear inner face of the receiver around the head of the firing pin. Extensive dry-firing will peen this area, and force the non-ferrous metal inward to jam the head of the firing pin. So, don't snap an alloy-receiver gun when it's empty.

Mainspring Tension

Many of the hammerless shotguns and rifles really should be called "internal hammer" guns, because they have a true pivoting hammer inside the receiver. In others, the hammer is actually a cylindrical piece that moves in the same plane as the bolt. And, there are some true hammerless guns, with a striker that moves in a tunnel in the bolt, having its front tip reduced to be the firing pin. Regardless of which of these three systems might be used, any time the action is cycled, the gun is cocked. For owners of these guns who are concerned about care, this presents a problem: Is it less harmful to leave the gun cocked during long storage, or to pull the trigger and snap it on an empty chamber?

As with most questions of this sort, there is no easy answer. There are differences in the quality of mainsprings, even in otherwise identical guns from the same maker. Blade-type springs are not used in many modern rifles and shotguns, and while springs of this type are not as prone to weakening from long compression, they do have more of a breakage frequency. Most modern rifles and shotguns have hammer or striker springs that are helical coil type, and most of these have ample power allowance for age-weakening. In some guns, though, this allowance is minimal, and compression for a long

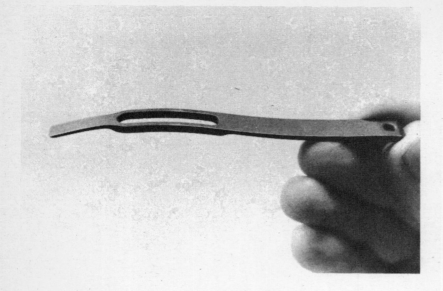

Blade-type springs, such as this hammer spring from a Browning A5 shotgun, are less susceptible to weakening from long compression, but they break more frequently.

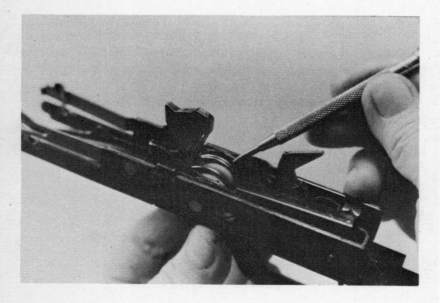

In most modern shotguns and rifles, hammer springs are of helical coil or torsion type, the latter shown here in a Winchester Model 1200 shotgun.

time may cause the spring to "take a set," as they say, and lose some of its power.

In practical use, this will show up in misfiring, with the hammer or striker failing to have enough impact on the firing pin to ignite the primer. If the gun in question is used primarily as a plinker, this is no great problem. If it happens, you can just have the spring replaced. If, however, the gun is a shotgun used as a police weapon, or for personal protection, a misfire could have serious consequences. If this situation occurs with a shotgun or rifle used mostly for hunting, it could mean lost game.

My own policy is to pull the trigger and drop the hammer. When I have a snap-cap in the proper caliber, then it is used. If I don't have one, I just reason that a very infrequent snapping is not as harmful as incessant dry-firing practice. If the gun is a 22 rifle, it's a good policy to insert a fired 22 caliber case, with the head turned so the firing pin will strike an unindented area. Thus, when the hammer fails, you have the same softened impact as in regular firing.

Some mainsprings will survive being compressed for long periods of time with no appreciable loss of tension. Others will take a set in a short time, and will cause misfiring until they are replaced. There is, unfortunately, no way to tell whether any particular spring will go one way or the other. So, if it's possible without unduly stressing the firing pins, my advice is to let the hammer or striker down. Use snap caps or an empty 22 case, whenever possible.

Magazines

Repeating rifles and shotguns will generally have one of two magazine types: Either an integral or removable box-type, or a tubular magazine law enforcement. These guns are kept fully loaded at all times, and the possibility of feeding being affected by a weakened magazine spring

When guns are used for home protection or in law enforcement, magazines are likely to be left fully loaded for long periods of time. In most cases, this will not weaken the magazine spring.

zine. The spring question is also important here: How much harm is done when a magazine is left fully loaded for long periods of time? This question will not be an essential one to those who use a shotgun or rifle only for hunting or recreational shooting, as their guns are loaded only when in actual use in the field. The magazines are empty when they are put away.

It becomes a real factor, though, when the gun is used for personal or home defense, or in is a serious concern. Over the years, I have encountered several instances of magazines that were left full for almost unbelievable periods of time—in 22 rifles and in shotguns that had been put away in an attic or closet and forgotten for many years. In every case, after the "aged" ammunition was removed and fresh cartridges or shells were tried, the gun fed and fired perfectly.

I mentioned earlier, in regard to mainsprings,

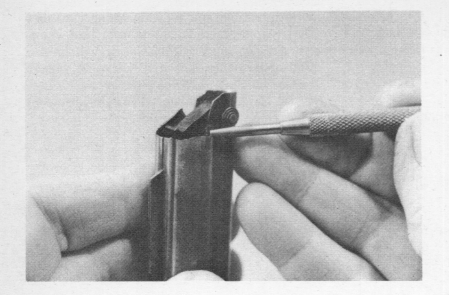

Amateur attempts to reshape magazine feed lips will often result in breakage, as on the Winchester Model 77 magazine shown. Magazine repair is a very specialized art.

Tubular magazines are fairly delicate, and should be handled with care, as even a slight bending or dent can cause misfeeding. Some, like the one shown, have plastic followers, and these have also been known to break.

that there was an extra tension-allowance in most firearms springs, and in the case of magazines, I've found that there is even more leeway. Among people that I know in law enforcement, there are two officers (they are in different cities) who have widely varying views on this question. Regarding the Remington Model 870 shotgun in the rack in each cruiser, each man follows his own pattern: One leaves it fully magazine-loaded at all times, the only

spring relief being when it is fired periodically at the police range, or in some serious social encounter. The other officer completely unloads the gun at the end of his shift, every night. Neither gun has ever failed to feed in 5 years of use. You can draw your own conclusions.

Box magazines that are detachable from the gun are susceptible to other types of damage. If the feed lips are deformed from the magazine being dropped on hard surfaces, or from slamming the magazine into its well in the gun, even a slight variation can cause it to misfeed. Most magazines, even though made of sheet steel, are relatively sturdy, but they should be given special care in handling.

When you encounter a magazine that someone else has abused, never attempt to adjust the feed lips with pliers. This will usually ruin the magazine, and if it's one of those with tempered feed lips, the result can be actual breakage. The best thing to do is to have the magazine examined by a gunsmith, and let him decide whether it should be replaced or repaired. Among the major components of a gun, the magazine is the least expensive part. Its cost is a very reasonable price for reliability. When misfeeding occurs, however, don't assume that it's always the magazine, as there are several other factors that may be involved.

Tubular magazines, in both shotguns and rifles, have an inside diameter that is only marginally larger than the rim diameter of the cartridges or shells used. So, even a slight dent can often stop a tubular magazine from functioning. It is sometimes possible to remove a tubular magazine dent, but in most cases, the tube may have to be replaced. In 22 rifles with removable inner magazine tubes, care should be taken to avoid bending.

Extractors and Ejectors

The terms above are often confused. In non-repeating shotguns and rifles, break-open types, the part located below the chamber that pushes the case out is called an ejector. In shotguns, this takes two forms—an ejector that just moves the shell out to be manually removed, and automatic ejectors that throw the shells clear. An extractor is normally located on the bolt, to the rear of the chamber, and it pulls the fired case out. Repeating rifles and shotguns have both an extractor and an ejector, but in this case the latter is a fixed or spring-powered part that kicks the empty case out the ejection port.

The ejectors of single and double barreled

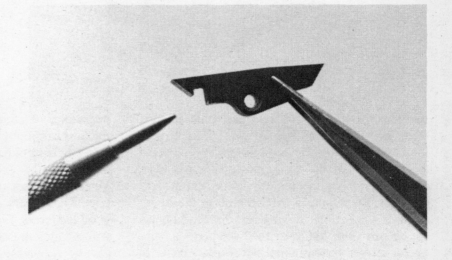

This shotgun extractor has a pronounced bevel on its beak, and single-loading of a gun with this type is not harmful, as the extractor can easily climb the rim of the case.

The ejectors in double-barreled shotguns are usually large and heavy parts, and breakage or malfunction is not an ordinary occurrence. Note the recess in the lower edge, designed to clear the firing pin as the action is opened.

The massive ejector used in quality single-barrels is also practically immune to any damage.

shotguns are usually massive parts that seldom break and require no special care. This is also frequently true of the fixed ejectors in repeaters, though some of the spring-powered types may occasionally require repair. Some extractors, however, do require a certain care in the operation of the action. A good example would be the classic 1898 Mauser rifle, which has an extractor with a very minimal bevel on its beak. It is designed for pickup of cartridges from the magazine, the rounds rising to engage the extractor beak, but the bolt will normally not close on a single round dropped into the chamber. If it is forced, the extractor beak can be broken. Since this is not the only gun in which the extractor has a very steep bevel on its beak, it is a good idea to be familiar with the extraction system in any gun that you use. If the action resists closing when single-loaded directly into the chamber, check to see how much bevel is on the

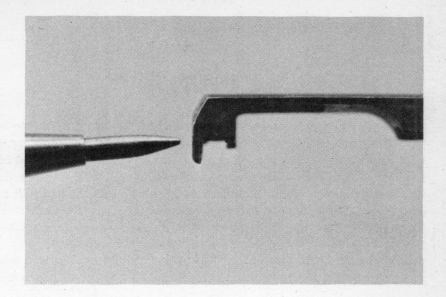

When the extractor beak has very little bevel, as on this Mauser-type, it is intended for proper engagement only when cartridges are fed from the magazine. Single-loading may not be possible, and if it's tried, may cause damage.

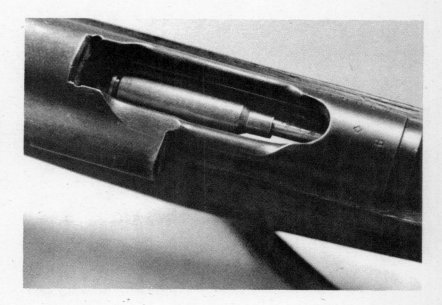

If the extractor fails to pull a fired case from the chamber, any attempt to pry it out at the rear is likely to mar the gun. The proper method, as shown, is to insert a rod from the muzzle, and push it out.

extractor beak. When this type of extractor design is encountered, be sure that loading is done only through the magazine, to avoid extractor damage.

When there are pronounced extraction or ejection difficulties, there are several mechanical conditions that can be blamed. These include roughness in the chamber, tired brass that fails to rebound after obturation, or, in the 22 rimfires, a dent at the edge of the chamber that has caused a protrusion inward. In all of these, the extractor or ejector is not at fault. Not realizing this, an amateur gunsmith will sometimes attempt to overcome one or more of these problems by installing a heavier spring to power the extractor. The result is usually a broken extractor beak. When a fired case is really stuck in the chamber, the only right way to remove it is to insert a rod from the muzzle and push it out. Then, consult a gunsmith.

Loose Screws

Rifle and shotgun shooters do not normally have the problem that is common to magnum-level handguns, screws loosening from recoil. Even so, it's a good idea to check all of the screws occasionally on any gun that is subject to a lot of use. Stock-mounting screws, especially, are subject to loosening from the effect of atmospheric changes on the wood. When shrinkage occurs, the action screws on a rifle stock may suddenly become loose. If this is not corrected,

bled several times, energetic tightening of these screws may have compressed their collars, allowing them to bear directly on the parts. In this case, when they are loosened to clear, rotation of the part will back them out further. If relieving the underside of the screw head will not restore the original clearance, they will have to be replaced.

On rifles, when tightening stock mounting screws that have loosened because of changes in

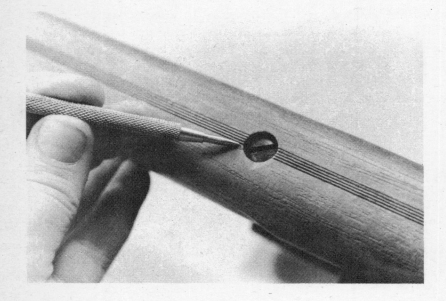

When tightening the large screws that hold the action in the stock, be sure that the inner tip of the screw does not bear on some portion of the mechanism and interfere with its operation.

and if the gun is a high-powered rifle with substantial recoil, the stock may even be cracked the next time it is fired. The same thing applies to shotguns that have a buttstock mounted with a bolt from the rear.

Any screw that retains a pivoting part is also subject to potential loosening. On 22 rifles, a good example might be the collared screws that retain the safety lever and its positioning spring in several guns. If the gun has been disassem-

the wood, take care that the inner tip of the mounting screw or screws will not interfere with any internal mechanism. On the Savage/Stevens Model 87A, for example, an over-tightening of the single large screw that retains the action in the stock can bring its tip into contact with the magazine tube, jamming the magazine in place. If the protrusion is far enough, the tube can even be damaged. A quick repair for this is to install a spacer washer under the head of the stock

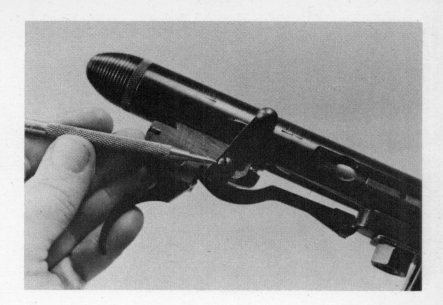

Any screw that retains and pivots a moving part is susceptible to loosening from normal functioning, and these should be checked with some frequency. Over-tightening should be avoided, as this can bind the movement of the part.

screw. The point, though, is to be sure when tightening any screw on a gun that its inner tip will not interfere with a part of the mechanism.

Some screws on rifles and shotguns are not machine screws, threaded into metal, but wood screws. When these are over-tightened, they can strip their holes in the wood. There are several old-time quick-fixes for this, such as a toothpick or steel wool in the hole, but the best repair is to fill the hole with Devcon 5-minute epoxy, let it cure, then re-drill the hole in a size that will allow snug tightening.

Safety Systems

The first thing to remember about the manual safety on any rifle or shotgun is that it should not be trusted. No matter how sophisticated the design, even if it meets all of the "state of the art" criteria so dear to the hearts of product liability lawyers, it cannot and must not be a substitute for safe gun handling practices. Like all of the other parts of a firearm, a safety is a mechanical device. Its components can break, or someone with enough strength may be able to over-ride its function. Some other part, not even connected with the safety, may break and allow the gun to fire. In a way, handling firearms is like handling explosives: Mistakes are not allowed.

With the foregoing in mind, let's look at some of the manual safety systems used on typical shotguns and rifles. There are two types of safety commonly used on shotguns. One is a cross-bolt push-button type, located just behind the trigger, or, sometimes, just in front of it. This type usually directly blocks movement of the trigger. The normal off-safe motion is toward the left, but reverse buttons are available for left-handed shooters. The other type is frequently seen on double-barreled or over/under shotguns, and on some slide-action shotguns, such as the Mossberg 500 series. It is an oblong or rectangular piece that is mounted on the upper tang or the rear extension of the receiver, and slides forward to off-safe. It also directly blocks trigger movement. On many double shot-

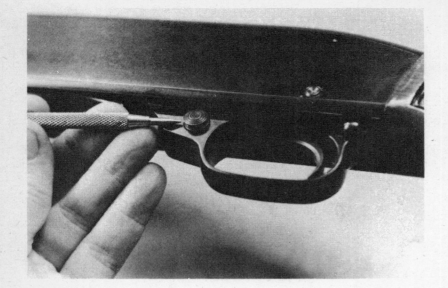

A frequently-used safety on shotguns is the cross-bolt push-button type, usually blocking movement of the trigger.

Military bolt action rifles of an earlier time often used the familiar flip-over Mauser-type safety. In the position shown, it blocked both the striker and the bolt.

guns, an internal bar moves the safety back to on-safe position automatically when the action is opened. Many trap and skeet shooters remove this actuator bar, with good reason. It's also possible that someone may have lost the little bar during disassembly, so don't depend on it always being there. Other than its automatic-on-safe-when-opening feature, it has no effect on the operation of the safety.

Rifle safety systems are much more varied.

Some have the trigger-block cross-bolt like the first of the two above, and a couple have the other shotgun-type safety. Many of the early military and sporting rifles used variations of the 1898 Mauser safety, a flipper that was mounted on the rear of the bolt. On most modern rifles, a popular choice seems to be on the right side at the rear of the receiver. This type is usually a lever or a sliding piece that internally blocks the sear. The direction of off-safe movement varies

Some bolt and striker blocking safety levers were located on the receiver, as on this British Enfield. It is shown in the on-safe position.

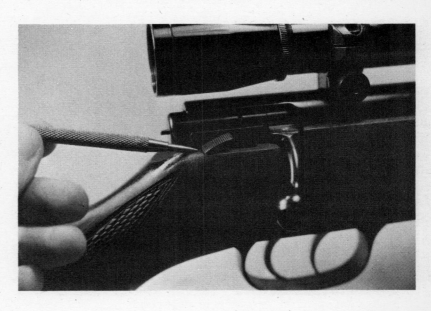

On many modern sporting rifles, the safety lever is positioned at the right rear of the receiver. On this Krico 22, it is shown on-safe.

with each gun. External-hammer rifles and shotguns have always had just a safety step (notch) on the hammer—a perfectly adequate arrangement. In recent years, though, some guns of this type have been made with manual hammer-block systems and transfer bars connected to the trigger.

The last two things mentioned have been added by lawsuit-wary manufacturers in an effort to make the gun unlikely to fire if dropped.

If the gun falls far enough, and the hammer is struck with enough force, both types can be over-ridden. I haven't dropped a rifle or shotgun in the 40 years I've been handling them, and I doubt that I ever will. To me, a safety is a device designed to prevent inadvertent firing by a pull on the trigger, not a thing to render a firearm totally harmless. You can depend on it to do what it was intended to do, but let's not ask too much of a mechanical device.

Carrying

In actual use in the field, the best way to carry a rifle—or a shotgun—is with a good sling. I know that shotgun slings are not popular in this country, as they are in Europe, but they should be. They make carrying less fatiguing, and would prevent many of the stumbling-with-a-gun accidents. This would not apply, of course, to shotguns used in duck and goose hunting, as those are usually carried to the blind in cases.

I just made a check of the slings on the rifles

City, Tennessee 38261). A sporterized Swiss Schmidt-Rubin, still in its original 7.5 x 55mm chambering, is wearing a black nylon Speed Sling from AMS Sales & Marketing, Inc. (1606 Oak Street Southeast, Salem, Oregon 97301). This is an innovative and unusual sling, with a square "ring" that is easily slid downward to lengthen the sling, or upward to tighten it. It's an ingenious design, and works perfectly. It can be used to carry in the usual sling position, on

Nylon slings are immune to several of the ailments that occur with leather, and they have become very popular. The one shown, in camouflage-pattern, is from Michaels of Oregon, also the source of the locking sling-swivels.

in one of my cabinets, to see what types I'm using. Two of them, on my Krico 22 rimfire and my Krico 22-250, are nylon, one black, and the other in camouflage. They're from Michaels of Oregon (Post Office Box 13010, Portland, Oregon 97213), and the latter is also on swivels from Michaels. My 9.3 x 57mm Husqvarna, with its mounted-on-the-barrel forward sling loop, has a European shotgun sling with ¾-inch ends that came from Dixie Gun Works (Union

the shoulder, or in lengthened mode it can sling the gun backpack fashion, vertically, in the center of the back, leaving both hands free for climbing or handling game. It's also available in top-grade leather. Write to AMS for the price.

Another interesting sling, one I've seen but haven't tried, is the Action Sling, marketed by Slings & Things, Inc., 8901 Indian Hills Drive, Suite 4, Omaha, Nebraska 68114. This one should do well for hunters, as it mounts the gun

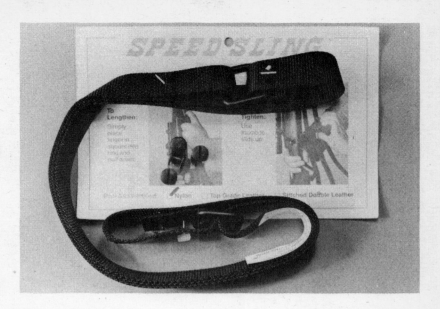

The Nylon Speed Sling has a sliding ring that allows quick adjustment of the sling length. It is also available in leather.

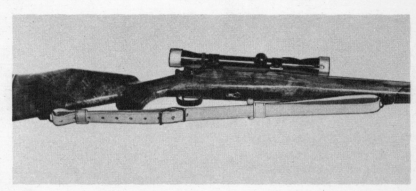

Brownells' well-known Latigo sling is of high-quality leather, and has several excellent features.

For the smaller-size loops of some European rifles and shotguns, Dixie Gun Works has this leather sling with narrower end-straps. It's of excellent quality, and is not expensive.

The Action Sling is shown in carrying position (above, left), unsnapped and in mid-movement (above, right), and in firing position (right). Its unique design is patented, and it is available in both nylon and leather.

diagonally across the front of the body, with the barrel pointing upward toward the shoulder. It leaves both hands free, and a snap lock tab by an upper ring keeps the gun snugged to the body. When hunting, the lock tab is unfastened, and the gun can be quickly turned and moved into firing position. It comes in two styles, plain and basketweave-pattern leather, and sells for around $30. There is also a nylon-web version.

There are many other good slings available. I mentioned shotgun slings earlier, and there are some available that require no hardware mounted on the gun. Two of the sources for this type are Eddie Bauer, 15010 NE 36th Street, Redmond, Washington 98052, and the Hunter Company, 3300 West 71st Avenue, Westminster, Colorado 80030. Here are some other sling sources:

Brownells, Inc.
Route Two, Box One
Montezuma, Iowa 50171

J. M. Bucheimer Co.
Postoffice Box 280
Frederick, Maryland 21701
The Eutaw Company
U. S. Highway 176W
Holly Hill, SC 29059
Pioneer Products
1033 West Amity Road
Boise, Idaho 83705

Nylon slings in camouflage-pattern are not unusual, but if you want one in *leather*, there's only one place to go: Ranger Leather Products, Post Office Box 3198, East Camden, Arkansas 71701. Or, if you should want a sling with your name custom-worked into the leather, get in touch with Kirkpatrick Leather Company, Post Office Box 3150, Laredo, Texas 78041. There are a lot more, of course, but that's all the space we'll take here on slings. If your gun has no sling loops or loop mounts, Michaels of Oregon has a huge array, for every purpose.

Cases

When the rifle or shotgun is not being carried for immediate use, and protection from dust or weather is wanted, some type of case will be needed. These can range all the way from the simple sheath to the hard cases that will withstand even the treatment of the gorillas who handle airline baggage. The sheaths mentioned above are made of a suede-like fabric or a soft plastic, and usually have an integral pair of tie-thongs at the end. They give mostly dust protection, but some will shed rain. Outers offers one that is impregnated with silicone, to be kind to the finish.

From the simple gun sheath, the next step upward would be the soft zipper case, with carrying handle. Some of these have the zipper opening across the large end and only half-way down, while others have a full-length zipper and

open out flat. They vary from regular gun shape to a wider type that will accommodate telescopic sights, and some are just rectangular. Materials are leather, soft plastic, and canvas or nylon. They are usually lined in flannel or a fur-like material, but some of the rectangular cases have linings of waffle-foam rubber.

In the relatively airtight cases of this type, such as those of soft plastic, it's not a good idea to store rifles or shotguns for long periods of time, no matter how well the metal surfaces of the gun may be protected by a preservative. Moist air can be trapped inside the case, and the moisture absorbed by the lining, which is in contact with the gun. A friend once put away a Remington 870 shotgun under these conditions for several months, and when it was taken out, it was badly rusted in several places.

A typical flannel-lined and vinyl-covered sheath is shown. Most of these have tie-thongs to secure the flap when the gun is inside.

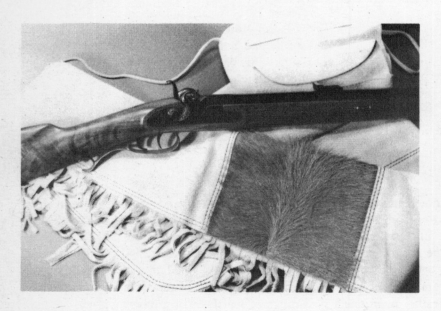

Here is a sheath of the same type, but much fancier. Designed for muzzle-loaders, it is made of suede leather, with fringe and a cowhide center panel.

There is one soft long-gun case that offers some protection against surface rust from moisture in the case. It's the new Gun Shield case by Bob Allen (214 S. W. Jackson Street, Des Moines, Iowa 50315). Inside this heavy-duty nylon case, which has a full-length zipper closure, there is a pocket that contains a packet of Hydroban 440, a powerful rust-inhibitor. After long use, the packets are replaceable. These nicely-made cases also have 1/2-inch foam padding, web handles, and tips of real leather. There is a color choice, silver with black trim, and brown with tan trim. They sell for around $45 to $47, depending on size.

A semi-rectangular case with waffle-foam lining that I use often is the #1120 from Special Weapons Products (Building 601, Space Center, Mira Loma, California 91752). It is 35 inches long, and will accommodate most carbine-length rifles, or full-length guns that have a

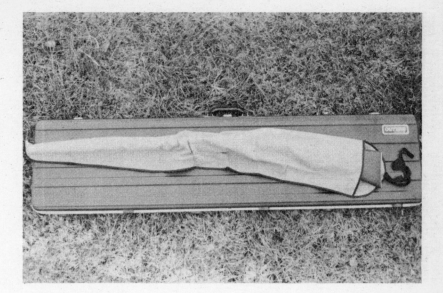

Outers furnishes this silicone-treated soft flannel sheath with their Silverline and hard plastic cases, and it is also available separately.

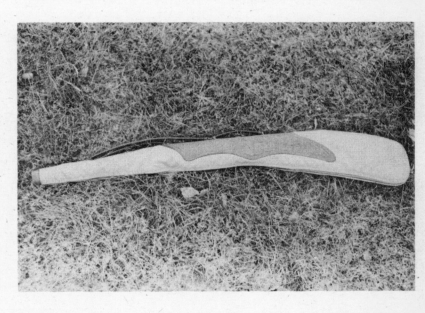

A typical vinyl zipper-type sheath, lined in flannel, with a carrying handle and shoulder strap. This is a very popular type.

folding stock. I frequently use it for my UZI carbine, along with the optional six-magazine holder that detaches to become a vest. These cases are particularly well-made, and come in sizes from 20 to 48 inches, with optional magazine or ammunition carrier-vests for 223 and 308 calibers, or 12 gauge shotgun.

Other cases are available from Special Weapons in different shapes, and the construction of all of them is a unique combination. The outer shell is 11-ounce waterproof Cordura nylon, and the closures are quiet YKK zippers and Fastex bucklers and hooks. Inside the outer shell is a layer of closed-cell Volara foam which not only makes the case semi-rigid, but will also make it float. The interior, as previously noted, is foam rubber in an egg-crate pattern. The case described, with the vest, has a retail price of just under a hundred dollars, and it is available without the vest for somewhat less. For a case of this

From Bob Allen, this padded nylon sheath is very well-made. In addition to a full-length zipper and carrying handle, it also contains a rust-inhibitor.

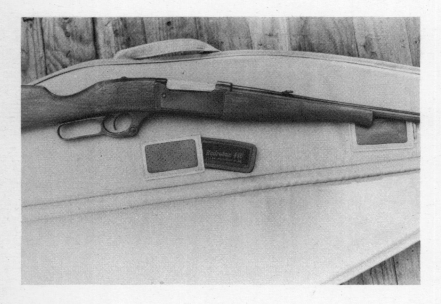

Inside the Bob Allen sheath are two pockets that house packets of Hydroban 440, to guard against rust.

quality and durability, the cost is reasonable.

I have owned and used many other regular soft rifle and shotgun cases, and have found that all of the ones with recognizable brand names lasted well and gave good protection. Some of the discount-store "no-name" cases that I've encountered do not hold up under hard use—the vinyl cracks, the zippers tend to come apart, and so on. So, it's smart to pay a bit more and get a quality case. I heard one horror-story about a cheap case: An experienced hunter, who should have known better, put his fine Browning Superposed in a no-name case that had an odd patterned flannel lining. Some chemical in the dyes used on the lining reacted with the plastic-based lacquer on his stock and forend, and totally ruined the finish on both.

The J. M. Bucheimer Company, mentioned earlier in regard to slings, also makes a line of excellent leather and vinyl cases. Brauer Broth-

This is a case from Special Weapons Products that I use often for assault rifles and semi-auto carbines. The exterior is of Cordura nylon, and the inside is lined in egg-crate foam rubber. A full-circumference heavy zipper allows it to open flat.

The Special Weapons case is shown open, with the UZI carbine. As you can see, it will also accomodate larger guns.

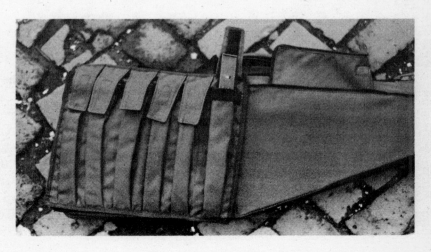

The rectangular left panel can be removed from the Special Weapons case, and stored in the zipper compartment on the right, as shown. In place of the panel, a magazine pouch can be zipped into place. Removed, the magazine carrier has straps that allow it to be worn as a vest. It is an optional accessory.

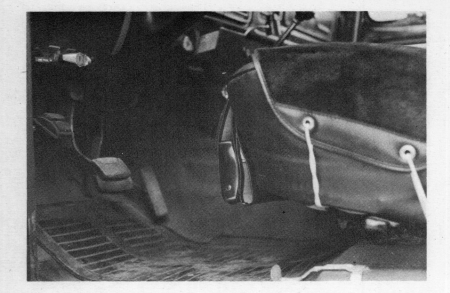

Shown on the front seat of my truck, the Lee Carrying case will hold two rifles or shotguns, inserted from opposite sides. The seat portion, in black "fur" on my case, is available in several variations. Nylon cord laces it to the seat.

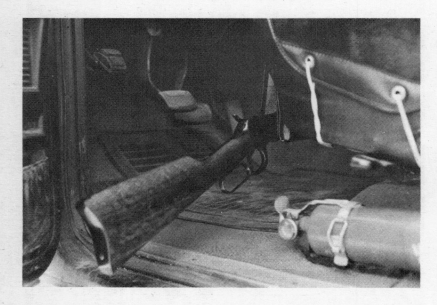

The Lee case is shown with the rifle partially removed. The weight of the gun holds it in place, so no closure is required. This is an excellent case, and a good value for its moderate price.

ers (817 North 17th, St. Louis, Missouri 63106) is well-known as a handgun holster maker, and also makes fine rifle and shotgun cases. Kolpin Manufacturing (Box 231, Berlin, Wisconsin 54923) makes a nice case of two-tone brown suede leather, and others. Another good line is by Boyt, a division of Welsh Sporting Goods, Box 1108, Iowa Falls, Iowa 50126. And, there are many others.

I recently installed an unusual and very handy soft case on the seat of my Ford Ranger pickup. It's called a Lee's Two-Gun Carrying Case, and it's made of heavy vinyl that covers the entire seat. The gun cases hang along the front edge of the seat, and are unobtrusive in that position. The openings of the cases are on each side, so the driver can remove his gun from his side, and a passenger from the other side. The unit laces in place with a tough nylon cord through grommets in the edges, and requires no alteration to

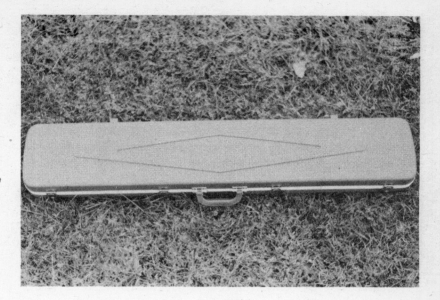

The deluxe Gun Guard case by Doskocil will accommodate a scoped rifle, and the plastic shell is thick and strong. The hinge is a full-length piano type, and the lining is waffle-foam rubber.

Here is the interior of the Gun Guard deluxe case. Note that there are four latches, two of them lockable.

the seat. It comes in a standardized brown vinyl for about $35, or in deluxe form in simulated lamb's-wool, of black, natural, or brown vinyl for $10 more. It's a well-made item, and works perfectly. The manufacturer is Whitehead Products Company, 1006 Meadow Lane, Fortuna, California 95540.

All of the soft cases described are fine for the carrying of rifles or shotguns on short journeys, as to the range or the hunting blind. For long-distance traveling, though, it's necessary to step up to the hard cases. These are fully lined in foam rubber, either smooth or in an egg-carton pattern. The lining grips the gun, or guns, firmly but gently, to keep them from moving if the case is jarred. This is important even in a motor vehicle, but when the case is to be transported by a baggage handler, it becomes an imperative.

The most economical of the hard cases is the

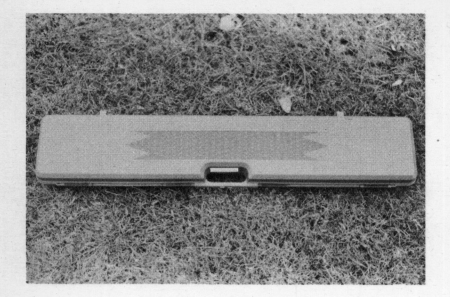

Designed to be used in the same way as a sheath, the less expensive Gun Guard case has no locking provision, but gives good protection.

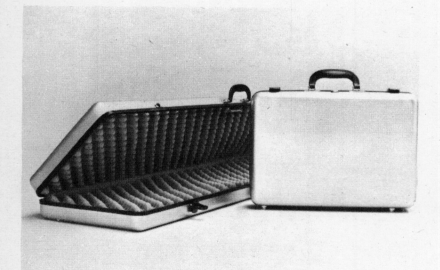

My favorite of the hard cases is the Outers Silverline, with an outer shell of formed aluminum. A rubber gasket seals the edges against weather, and the full-length piano hinge is covered in the same high-quality foam rubber as the lining. It locks with a machined key. The handgun-sized Silverline case is also shown.

plastic type, and these are remarkably durable. I have used two of these, and both have performed well. One is a Gun Guard case by Doskocil Manufacturing Company (Box 1246, Arlington, Texas 76010). It is a single-gun type, 48 inches long, and has ample width for a scoped rifle. The plastic shell is thick and sturdy, and the metal hinge is a full-length piano-type. The lining is waffle-foam. There are four efficient latches, two of which are lockable

with the same key (two keys are provided).

The Gun Guard line also offers a more economical case, made of the same tough plastic, which has four sliding latches and does not lock. It has four separate hinges of integral plastic, with steel pin centers. The lining is the same waffle (egg-carton?) foam. This is a good, solid case, but its lack of a locking feature would rule it out as a baggage item for long-distance travel. For use between home and the field, though, it

This large plastic case by Outers is particularly well-made. It has egg-carton foam lining, a full-length piano-type hinge that is vinyl-shielded, and locking latches. Its sturdy feet are screw-attached and replaceable.

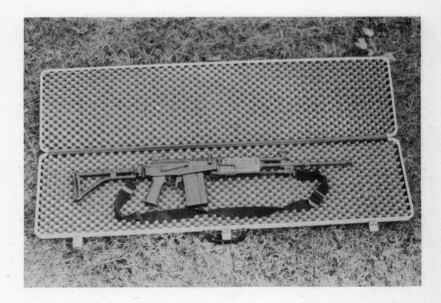

offers more protection than the soft cases.

My other deluxe plastic case is by the Outers Division of Omark Industries (Box 856, Lewiston, Idaho 83501). This is a two-gun case, 52½ inches long and 13 inches wide, and its construction is a combination of heavy plastic and aluminum alloy. A wide strip of the alloy surrounds the edges of the lid and bottom, and there are three latches, the outer two lockable with the same key (two provided). The full-

length piano-type hinge is internally shielded by a strip of vinyl, to prevent any chance of metal touching the guns. The sturdy feet are screw-attached and replaceable.

The plastic hard cases are fine, and are very resistant to damage. If you want to go first class, though, and impress the peasants, get an Outers Silverline. The two-gun case has the same dimensions as the case just above, but it's made entirely of formed aluminum, with a

A custom-built case by Wilson Case, Inc., of Juniata, Nebraska, this one is of heavy plywood, aluminum, and steel, and is virtually indestructible. Two of the four latches are lockable.

On the inside, the Wilson case has three layers of plain foam in the lower section, and waffle-foam in the lid. There is a full-length piano-type hinge, and lid supports unfold and lock on each side. Made to your specifications, this case is expensive, and worth it.

beautiful satin finish. When this case is new, it's almost too pretty to use. The first few times I took it out to the range, I spread a blanket in the back of the truck for it to lie on! Its features match its appearance. It has a full-length piano hinge that is internally covered in foam rubber, and has two manual latches and a fully-recessed lock with a machined key. The edges of the lid and bottom have a rubber gasket that seals against the weather, and the feet are also of aluminum—they won't crack or break off. This case has an ''approved'' airline rating, and the aluminum body is definitely not flimsy, but it's surprisingly light. Inside every new Silverline case, Outers packs one of the silicone-treated sheaths mentioned earlier. Also, this case costs a lot less than you might expect. The only way to top the Silverline is to go to a custom-built case, so let's look at one of those.

In the autumn of 1981, I traveled to Vermont

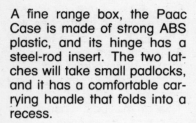
A fine range box, the Paac Case is made of strong ABS plastic, and its hinge has a steel-rod insert. The two latches will take small padlocks, and it has a comfortable carrying handle that folds into a recess.

and managed to terminate a 175-pound Russian boar before he did the same to me. The gun used was a Heckler & Koch HK91 A-2, with a 4-power Schmidt & Bender scope in a quick-detachable mount. Both the scope and the sights on the rifle were carefully set before the trip, and I wanted to make sure that neither got bumped out of alignment. The case I used was custom-made by Wilson Case, Inc., of Juniata, Nebraska 68955, a company that also makes specialized cases for delicate equipment used by government agencies. Constructed of heavy plywood and aluminum, my case measures 48 by 16 by 6 inches, and is acturally large enough for two average shotguns or rifles.

Everything about this case is stronger than necessary. It has a full-length piano-type hinge, and folding support arms on each side that lock to hold the lid open. There are four manual latches, two of them lockable, and the edges of the lid and bottom are tongue-in-groove to keep out dust and rain. All of the corners are completely sheathed in heavy-gauge nickel-plated steel. The lid is lined in egg-carton foam, and the bottom has three layers of smooth foam, to allow cutting out contours for nesting, if this is wanted. I've never weighed this case, but with the HK91 and its accessories inside, it is really *heavy*. On the other hand, it would doubtless survive being run over by a Jeep. This is a superb case. Made to each owner's specifications, it is expensive—and it's worth it.

Before we leave the subject of cases, some mention should be made of an item that protects your shooting accessories and ammunition, the range box. Those who shoot handguns often have elaborate and expensive range boxes, some with padded racks that keep several handguns neatly in a line. There are many times, though, when a range box can be a valuable accessory for the rifle or shotgun shooter, and I recently discovered one that is inexpensive, completely waterproof, and adaptable to the needs of either handgunners or long-gunners. It's called the Paac Case, and it's made by the West Ohio Gun Company, Incorporated (P-685 RD 16, Route Two, Napoleon, Ohio 43545) Constructed of tough ABS plastic, this case has an abundance of good features. A full-length hinge has a steel-rod center, and the equally-sized lid and bottom are designed to open out flat. Inside the lid, there is a lock-in "tray" that conceals a compartment lined in egg-carton foam rubber. While this feature was probably designed with handguns in mind, it could easily be used for a spare scope, and will actually contain (with the long

The lid and bottom of the Paac Case have the same dimensions, and it opens flat. The lid has a snap-in compartment lined in egg-carton foam rubber, and in the lower section are numerous compartments and a lift-out tray. This is the best case of its type that I have seen.

barrel removed) an UZI carbine.

The bottom of the Paac Case has three compartments. On the right, there is a large space suitable for earmuff-style hearing protectors, shooting glasses, and other items. At the rear on the right, there is a narrower bin for tools. The left side has a deep compartment with a lift-out tray that has a retractable handle, and the tray is divided. There is also space under the tray. The case has two latches that will take small padlocks, and the comfortable carrying handle folds flat into a recess. This range box is the best of its type I've ever seen, and comes with a 1-year guarantee.

''Care'' applies not only to guns, but also to those who shoot them. Back when I started fooling around with guns (no dinosaur jokes, please. . .) hardly anyone wore shooting glasses or hearing protectors. Today, all of those who are serious shooters use both. The effect of repeated loud noises on the auditory nerves has been proven, so some type of ear guard against the sound of gunfire just makes good sense. I mostly use the earmuff type, and I usually keep spares on hand (hanging on the rifle rack in the truck) for anyone who might be at the range with me, without a set.

My extras include muffs by Clark and Si-

lencio, but the set I personally use is the Viking #2318, made by Bilsom AB of Billesholm, Sweden. Among the regular foam-lined muffs, these are the most effective and most comfortable I've found. The EPA rates various hearing protectors on noise reduction, on a scale of 0 to 30. The Viking muffs are rated at 28. I usually wear them in the behind-the-head position, and these muffs are not only adaptable to this, but they also have an extra touch: There's an adjustable soft plastic strap that will go over the top of the head, and it's removable if it isn't needed or wanted. The main band that the muffs are mounted on is deeply padded with foam that's covered in soft plastic. This is a quality earmuff, and for its features, the price is reasonable.

Shooters who do not wear prescription glasses should always wear shooting glasses. Even with the best guns in fine condition, there is always a chance that some quirk of the gun or an energetic handload might send some powder gases back toward the shooter, or even a few tiny pieces of metal. With semi-autos, an ejected case from the gun of a fellow shooter can inflict injury, if it strikes an eye. Blackpowder shooters, whether using flintlock or caplock, should especially beware of sparks or pieces of percussion caps.

I wear prescription glasses, but I don't use

The Bilsom Viking hearing protector has a foam-padded frame and a strap of soft plastic that can be worn over the head. I use this particular set of earmuffs most of the time.

My shooting glasses are by Bilsom/Uvex, made of high-quality polycarbonate with steel temple-pieces. Mine are yellow, but they also come in clear and in grey.

them on the range. Neither my reading nor driving glasses are right for looking at sights, so I use yellow-lens shooting glasses. By a coincidence, they are the fine Uvex-made Rangemasters, marketed by Bilsom, the maker of my earmuffs. In yellow, they're Model #1161, but they are also offered in grey and clear. The lenses are made of heavy polycarbonate, and they easily pass the A. N. S. I. standard for shatter-resistance. The temples are steel, with vented side-shields, and the ear-hooks are comfortable plastic. The steel temple hinges are screw-mounted. These are high-quality glasses, and come with a nice nylon case with a belt loop.

As with the earmuffs, I also keep a spare set of shooting glasses in my range box, and those are by Hoppe's (their #3070). Except for the steel temple-hinges, they are made entirely of polycarbonate, and the temples have integral side-shields. Although these glasses are very inexpensive, they also comply with all of the safety standards. For more information on these, write to Hoppe's Division, Penguin Industries, Airport Industrial Mall, Coatesville, Pennsylvania 19320. The Hoppe's glasses also come in a case of hard plastic. Like the others, they also are available in clear and in grey.

Safety

The most important aspect of firearms care is not mechanical maintenance, it's safe handling. A few years back, someone at the Sporting Arms and Ammunition Manufacturers Institute came up with a list of rules that came to be known as the "Ten Commandments of Safety." The list has been repeated, with some variations, by the National Shooting Sports Foundation, the National Rifle Association, and several manufacturers. Some readers may have joined us recently, so I'll repeat the original rules one more time:

1. Treat every gun with the respect due a loaded gun.

2. Carry only empty guns, taken down or with the action open, into your automobile, camp, or home.

3. Always be sure that the barrel and action are clear of obstructions.

4. Always carry your gun so that you can control the direction of the muzzle, even if you stumble.

5. Be sure of your target before you pull the trigger.

6. Never point a gun at anything you do not intend to shoot.

7. Never leave your gun unattended unless you unload it first.

8. Never climb a tree or a fence with a loaded gun.

9. Never shoot at a flat hard surface or the surface of water.

10. Do not mix gunpowder and alcohol.

These are still good rules, especially when they are applied to target shooting, plinking, or hunting. In some homes, though, rifles or shotguns are used for purposes of protection, and in that case, some of the rules quoted above would not logically apply. For protective purposes, a handgun is really the best choice. The long barrel of a shotgun or rifle is a liability in close quarters, and centerfire ammunition penetrates walls too easily to be safely fired inside a house. In some localities, though, the ownership of handguns is heavily regulated, often to the point that the use of one in self defense would leave the homeowner in more legal difficulty than the criminal. Also, in many rural areas, a shotgun or rifle is an all-around tool, used to put meat in the freezer, and to discourage predators, animal or human. When a rifle or shotgun is the first line of defense, strictly observing rules number two and seven could make you a victim. You can imagine the scenario: You are startled out of sleep after midnight by the sound of breaking glass, and hear muffled voices, then footsteps on the stairs. In the dark, you have to quickly find the cartridges or shotgun shells, and load the gun. The intruders are now at the door of your bedroom. Will you make it in time?

The Master Gun Lock is well-known, and uses a machined key. When applied to a rifle or shotgun as shown, the gun cannot be fired until its removal.

Any gun that is a primary piece for home defense must be quickly accessible, and *loaded*. When the household consists only of knowledgeable adults, this presents no problem, other than to always warn visitors about it. When there are children, though, it's obvious that a loaded gun can't just be left lying around. There are three ways to handle this problem, and no single one of them is a total answer. Sometimes, when the children involved are very small, it's best to use all three: Lock-up, choice of gun, and instruction.

When certain guns are used only for hunting or other sporting purposes, then of course they should be kept unloaded, and locked up in a gun cabinet or closet. For defense purposes, though, this arrangement fails to meet the necessary requirements. So, for those who choose the lock-up method, we go to the next best thing: Load the shotgun or rifle, keep it in an accessible spot, and lock only that gun. This is possible, when you use the Master Model 90 Gun Lock, made by the Master Lock Company of Milwaukee, Wisconsin, and available at most gun shops and sporting goods stores. It's padded with soft rubber to prevent any marring of the gun, and fits over the entire trigger guard. It locks with a removable key, and the key can be kept in a handy but well-hidden place, known only to the adults in the family. When the Master Gun Lock is properly installed on any rifle or shotgun that is in proper working order, it is virtually impossible for the gun to be fired. If a serious situation occurs, finding and operating a single key is a lot easier and quicker than fumbling with ammunition in the dark. The company, of course, says that it should not be used on loaded guns. This unit is well-made, and costs less than $10.

There is another device available that is even more economical, and requires no key. It's called the "Agapē Gun Lock," and it consists of nylon cable ties, plastic T-blocks, and a steel break ring. While it's designed for use only on empty guns, it works by blocking the action open, and it would be possible to keep a full magazine in readiness and use this device. I should point out that this is *my* reasoning, not the manufacturer's. In use, the action is opened, the T-bar inserted (in some cases, just the tie is used), and the cable tie is threaded through and locked to prevent operation of the action.

To remove the nylon cable tie, there are two options. It can be cut, with some difficulty, with scissors or a knife. Or, when installing the cable tie, you can run it through the steel emergency

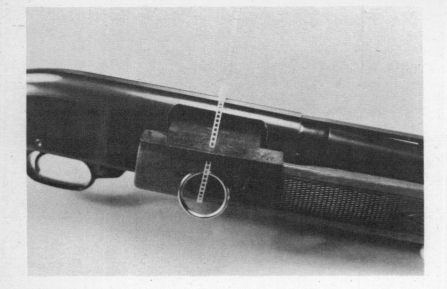

Nylon cable ties are the main element of the Agapē Gun Lock. The deluxe kit includes plastic T-bars in three sizes and an emergency break ring. The lock is shown installed in a slide-action shotgun.

This little tag of red plastic is called a Tattle-Tale. It does not prevent the gun from being fired, but it is a good warning for those who might forget.

break ring that comes with the kit. A sharp twist of the ring will break the tie. It has been determined that this takes 60 pounds of force, and this is beyond the hand strength of most children, but relatively easy for an adult. Two Agapē kits are available. One has just ten of the nylon ties and a break ring, and the other has the same items and three T-blocks. The kits are quite inexpensive. The address is: Agapē Gun Lock, Incorporated, Box 11, Belmont, MI 49306.

There is one more inexpensive and useful device that I want to mention. It won't lock up a gun like the two just described, but used in homes where there are no small children, it will warn the forgetful. It's a little red plastic clip that will easily snap onto the trigger guard of any rifle or shotgun, and on both rectangular sides (1 by 1½ inches) it says in large white letters: CAUTION: LOADED FIREARM. Its maker, John Stupero (Box 155, Lakeville, Min-

The pistol-caliber semi-auto carbines are good choices for home defense. Most of them have fairly strong bolt springs, and with loaded magazine and empty chamber could be child-safe. And, their appearance is an asset. From the left, the ones shown are the Thompson M27A-1, Wilkinson Terry, Demro XF7 Wasp, UZI, and Commando M45.

nesota 55044), calls it the Tattle-Tale. In an emergency, the gun could still be fired, without the tag being removed. For their intended purpose, these little things are an excellent idea.

Now, let's look at the second point I mentioned, the choice of guns. Many modern shotguns and rifles have beautifully smooth actions, as they should have for easy operation in the field. Some of them, though, could also be worked, with some effort, by a sturdy child. With many guns, this rules out the otherwise excellent idea of just loading the magazine, and leaving the chamber empty. There are a few guns, however, in which this arrangement would work. The old Winchester Model 1897 slide action shotgun, for example, requires an effort for operation that even some adults find difficult.

Among today's slide action and semi-auto shotguns, there are none that have enough difficulty of operation that I would think of them as a possible choice for this application. Some models of the classic Browning A5 might be acceptable, the ones that have a manual magazine cut-off lever. With the magazine filled, the cut-off could be set in ''off'' position, blocking feeding. Also, if a child managed to open the breech it would lock open, and then would re-

quire knowledge of the release button to close it.

Double or single-barreled shotguns have either easily-operated manual safety systems or external hammers, and so should not be left loaded and unattended in child-accessible places. On the other hand, they are relatively easy to load when trouble threatens, so keeping the shells inaccessible but handy could be the answer here. Most centerfire and rimfire rifles—those with integral magazines—also have actions that are easily operated. The ones that have detachable box magazines are a good choice—just load the magazine, and keep it in a separate place. Inserting it and cycling the action would take only seconds.

There is one type of gun that is particularly well-suited for home, farm or ranch defense: The pistol-caliber semi-auto carbine. These are mostly in 45 Auto or 9mm Luger chambering, and they include such guns as the Thompson, Demro, Terry, and Commando, and the semi-auto version of the UZI. These carbines are relatively short and easy to handle, and they have magazine capacities of 20 to 30 rounds. And, they *look* like submachine guns, so their very appearance would likely be intimidating to an intruder. For child safety, removal and separate storage of a loaded magazine would be effec-

The age at which firearms instruction should be begun can be determined only on an individual basis. When this photo was made, Ethan was 6 years old, and was already well-versed in the safe handling of firearms.

tive. If the children are very small, the strong bolt springs of these guns would probably prevent their operation, even with the magazine in place.

When we consider homes with older children, it brings us to the last point mentioned—Instruction. Most of the accidents with firearms that occur in the home are the result of the natural inquisitiveness of children in the age range of 5 to 12. In homes where a gun of any type is kept for protection, the first thing to do is to satisfy the child's curiosity. Show the child how the gun works, and especially how to check to see whether it is loaded. Stress that even after it has been shown to be unloaded, it still is never to be handled without an adult present, and not to be pointed toward another person. When the child is old enough to properly hold the gun, take him or her out to a range and let them shoot the gun. If all of this is done right, it will remove the mystery of the gun, and will also serve as an introduction to the great sport of shooting.

From a very early age, all of my children have been surrounded by guns, and they have been carefully taught proper handling. A couple of years ago, my son Ethan, who was then 10, was standing at the pistol cabinet, holding a handgun. He had just removed the magazine and checked the chamber to determine that it was unloaded, and was aiming it across my office at a wall. I was at my desk, talking to my friend Steve Robbins, who was seated on the other side of the cabinet, beyond Ethan. Steve stood up to come over to the desk, and Ethan instantly brought down the hand holding the gun, turned back toward the cabinet, and kept the gun pointed at the floor while Steve passed by. This, without a word being spoken.

Incidents like this show why my children are not likely to ever have an accident with a firearm. It should be noted, though, that no matter how well you train the members of your own household, there is still a danger of mishandling by a visitor, and this applies not only to small friends of your child, but also to adult visitors who are not knowledgeable about guns. In regard to this, keep in mind that the responsibility, both morally and legally, is yours. If you keep a rifle or shotgun for protection, take appropriate precautions.

Storage

One of the first things that comes to mind, when considering the proper storage of rifles and shotguns, is the possibility of theft. We are often told that gun owners should not display their firearms in locations where they can be seen from outside. Some security experts also advise against glass-front gun cabinets, recom-

mending that all firearms be stored in concealed safes or safe-like cabinets. Some further advise that gun owners should not show their guns to anyone, even friends, so it won't become known that they have firearms. In certain high-crime areas, I can see that all of these admonitions might be good advice.

This Outers Stowline steel cabinet will accomodate five rifes or shotguns, and has shelves on the right for ammunition, handguns, or other accessories.

The eight-gun Stowline model has a small shelf at the top, and a handy ammo-bin on the door. These cabinets are made of heavy-gauge welded steel, and are lined in foam-laminated brushed nylon.

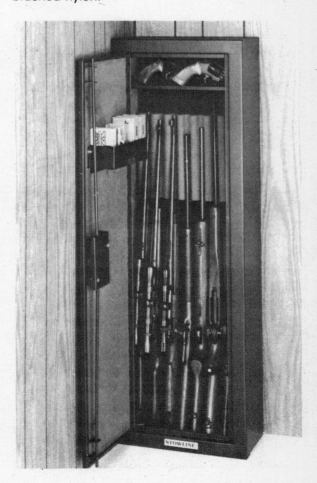

This Stowline holds ten rifles or shotguns, has a small top shelf, and a two-shelf bin on the door. Note the two heavy latching rods and the shielded lock area.

I'm very fortunate, in being able to ignore all of these warnings. I live in a very small community in western Kentucky, and around here, a major break-in would be front-page news. As a well-known "gun person," I could hardly pretend that there were no firearms here. My working hours are unusual, from 8 or 9 in the evening to 3 or 4 in the morning, and if anyone were skulking about, my dogs would let me know. The inside dog is a Dachshund who would not hesitate to attack a Cape Buffalo, and

there is always a firearm of some sort within reach. It would be difficult to surprise me. No one has tried.

I'm aware, though, that most of this would not apply to the average homeowner or urban apartment-dweller. Most would have to decide on some form of security. The ultimate means, of course, would be a safe, and there are several fine ones offered, by Cannon, Fort Knox, Browning, Outers and others, that are specifically made for firearms. The cost is substantial, but for those who can afford them, vaults of this type can deter the common house-breaker. They might even delay a professional thief long enough to be caught or scared away.

In between the true vault-type safes and the regular gun locker, there is a lighter safe that offers good protection for much less cost. A fine example of this type is the Stowline, offered by the Outers Division of Omark Industries (Box 856, Lewiston, Idaho 83501). There are models that hold from five to ten rifles and shotguns, with varying arrangement of shelves. They lock with dual vertical rods and a machined key, and can be bolted to the wall. The outside is heavy-gauge welded steel, and the inside is lined in soft foam, laminated with brushed nylon. The largest measures 10 by 20 by 56 inches. Outers also offers a behind-the-seat Stowline unit for pickup trucks, made to the same standards. These are superb safes.

While the Outers Stowline units are reasonably priced for their quality, there may be those who might be looking for something even more economical, and I have it, sitting here in the corner of my office. It's a gun locker made by Medart, Incorporated (Box 658, Greenwood, Mississippi 38930), a company that is also known for making the tough lockers for schools. I have the Deluxe unit, which has space in its lower section for six shotguns or rifles, their barrels cradled in an appropriately-shaped bar covered in soft plastic. The bottom of the unit is covered in a plastic material that is like Astro-Turf, or indoor-outdoor carpet.

This is not a safe, but its construction is defi-

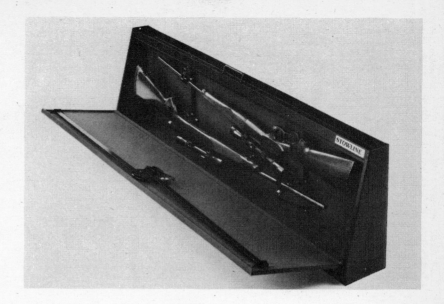

Outers also has a Stowline unit that fits neatly behind the seat of a pickup truck, and holds two guns, with space at the bottom for ammunition or accessories.

nitely not flimsy. The body parts are of 16, 18, and 24-gauge steel, finished in an attractive electrostatically baked-on enamel. The locker measures 72 by 18 by 12 inches. As they say with the Christmas toys, "assembly required," but I noted with pleasant surprise that all of the parts were there, and all of the holes were perfectly aligned. At the top of the locker, inside, there is a large shelf, and a separate inner compartment with a lockable door. This could be used for handguns, but I use it to store ammunition. The latches on the main door and the inner compartment door are an easily-operated lift-type, and both have a loop for a padlock. It's a fine locker, and at the time this is written, it sells for under $200, including shipping cost.

Wherever guns are in storage, whether in a safe, locker, or just a closet, humidity can be a serious problem, especially in some areas. My location is the western Ohio River Valley, and here it's definitely a thing to be considered. If the storage space is airtight, there is always the chance that condensation might occur. Active dehumidifiers powered by electricity are good, but there is the problem of getting the wiring into the storage unit. With the vault-type safes, this could be a big problem. I prefer to use passive dehumidifiers, the type containing silica gel

I use the shelf and the top compartment of the Medart locker entirely for ammo storage, but it could also be used for storage of handguns or other accessories. The locker is moderately-priced, and of excellent quality.

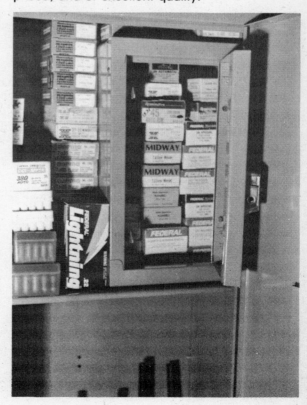

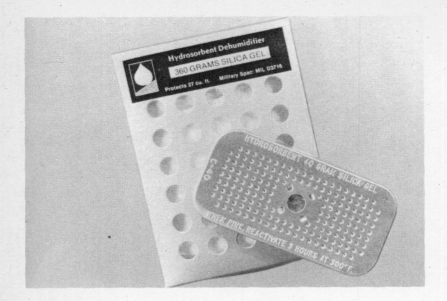

Large Hydrosorbent units are available for entire gun cabinets. The 40-gram and 360-gram units shown are for protective use in smaller closed areas, such as cabinet drawers.

These units by Rust Patrol use the same silica gel crystals as all dessicants of this type. The larger units have an indicator spot that changes color when the crystals need to be reactivated. This can be done in an ordinary kitchen oven.

crystals. This type of dessicant is at its best in tight enclosures, and it is used often by U. S. Government agencies, museums, and manufacturers. In the usual form, the silica gel crystals are in containers of varying size, and these are used according to the volume of the area to be protected. Containers may be of vented metal or cardboard, or a simple cloth bag. The larger units have an indicator panel that will change color when the crystals are saturated with mois-

ture. Then, the silica gel can be removed from the container and dried in the kitchen oven. If you continue to do this according to the instructions, these dehumidifiers can be used indefinitely.

I regularly use units from two sources. One is the Hydrosorbent Company (Box 675, Rye, New York 10580). Their 40-gram metal-cased type is in my pistol case on the wall, as it's suitable for smaller areas. In my Medart locker,

I use their 360-gram unit, which has a cloth bag in a vented cardboard box. This one protects 27 cubic feet of area. Hydrosorbent also offers units ranging up to a 2000-gram metal cylinder that will cover 144 cubic feet.

I also use silica gel dehumidifiers by Rust Patrol (6245 Rosier Road, Canandaigua, New York 14424), and several of their small disposable bags are in the drawers of my pistol cabinet. They also have a small metal-cased unit that is very much like the one described above, plus a large cloth drawstring bag that will cover 25 to 30 cubic feet of space and is renewable. The disposable units mentioned are made to be used for a specific time and then thrown away, but it

would be possible to open the little bags and heat-dry the crystals in them, just as in the others.

All of these dessicant-type dehumidifiers do a fine job, but it should be noted that they are not designed to dry out the entire room. They will work best and last longest when they are used in a tightly sealed enclosure. If they are in a storage space that is opened frequently, and the outside humidity is high, then they will have to be reactivated more often. When it's first used, a unit will deactivate more quickly than in later use, as it will be absorbing residual moisture in the structure or lining of the enclosure.

Alarm Devices

Let's backtrack for just a moment to the subject of preventing theft, and consider the electronic alarm systems. When the cost is not a major factor, there are very sophisticated and elaborate alarm systems available, but they are expensive. These include in-house units, and systems connected to law enforcement or security agencies. Feeling that the substantial cost of these units put them out of reach for the average gun-owner, it was my original intention to leave them out of this book. However, I have just tried and neat little unit that costs less than a hundred dollars, and works beautifully.

It's called the Owl, Model 200, and it's made

The Owl Model 200 by Web Electronics is a proximity-type alarm that will trip regardless of how quietly an intruder may move. It is a relatively inexpensive and very effective alarm.

by Web Detection, Incorporated (2000 Shames Drive, Westbury, New York 11590). This is not a sound detector, it's a proximity device that detects any movement within 20 feet, in any direction. It's not a toy-like plastic thing, but is heavy and well-made, definitely a high-quality electronic unit. Two 9-volt alkaline batteries are supplied with the ''Owl,'' and they'll last about a year, in normal use. A siren-type speaker is in the basic unit, but there is also a provision for plugging in an optional horn that can be placed away from the unit. My own Owl has the extra horn, and I think anyone using this device should have it. You can put the horn up near the ceiling or even outside the room, away from the sensor, and this would make it more difficult for an intruder to locate the device and silence the alarm by smashing it. This, by the way, is the only way it could be stopped, as it turns on and off with a removable machine-cut key. When it's first turned on, there is a delay of around 20 seconds, which allows you to get out of the room. Anyone who comes in and moves around after that will activate the alarm in 10 seconds.

When I was first testing the Owl, my sons had a good time trying to sneak quietly by it. Even when they crawled by on the floor, it triggered every time. The siren in the sensor unit is adequate, but the remote horn is even better, emitting a shriek that actually is painful to the ears. It can be heard through a closed door, upstairs, even outside. Most intruders would likely be frightened away when the siren is triggered. Even if they weren't, it would at least alert the household. We rarely leave the castle unattended, but on the occasion when everyone will be out of the house, I set the Owl. Even if the siren shriek doesn't frighten away an intruder, my good neighbor will hear it, and come over—with a shotgun.

Evaluation and Insurance

If you own only one gun, you should write down the make, model, and serial number, and keep this note in a safe place, separate from the gun. It would also be a good idea to put down the original price or current cash value of the gun. If you have several guns, or a collection, this information becomes even more important. The best way to get an evaluation of your guns is to have a professional appraisal done. If the guns are in a fire, or are stolen, or if you should suddenly depart this life, you'll get back the appraisal fee, many times over. Most insurance companies will use a professional appraisal to set the amount you'll receive in reimbursement for your loss. Quite a few of the appraisals that I have done were at the request of insurance firms.

If your guns are all of modern manufacture, you can often get a fair appraisal of their replacement cost at your local gun shop. Make it plain, when you are asking for an evaluation, that your guns are not for sale, and this will protect you from the possibility that a dishonest evaluator might assign a low value to some piece, then try to buy it. Another potential problem is an appraiser who may over-value the guns, with the idea of making his fee larger. You can guard against this by knowing the reputation of your appraiser, and by having a general idea of the approximate value of your guns. When I do an appraisal, I base my fee on three things: The amount of research involved, the number of guns, and the total value of the collection.

Remember that the value of any shotgun or rifle will depend on several factors. Among these are Condition, Scarcity, and Demand. You can apply these points to any gun, whether it's a collector piece or a firearm for practical use. In the latter department, a good used Winchester Model 70 rifle or a Browning A5 shotgun will always bring respectable prices, because both are guns that are popular with shooters and hunters. Conversely, in the collector field, I've seen some rare and beautiful German single-shot rifles sold for very reasonable prices, because the collector interest in these is low. It should also be noted that some tiny marking on a collector piece that denotes a scarce variation can often make a large difference in value.

In case of loss, your regular homeowner's insurance will usually cover a single gun. If, however, you have a number of valuable firearms, this will usually require a rider on your policy that will list each gun individually, and this will cost extra. If you are a member of the NRA, the Association offers a good insurance plan for this. If you're not a member, you should be. The address is: National Rifle Association, 1600 Rhode Island Avenue N. W., Washington, DC 20036. Fine firearms are a good investment and a valuable asset, comparable to your home, automobiles, and other property, and it just makes good sense to have them protected by insurance.

Gunsmithing

Excellent repair jobs are often done by experienced and knowledgeable shooters who are also skilled with tools. However, I have also seen many instances of poorly-fitted factory replacement parts, crude home-made parts, and rifles and shotguns that have been damaged by repair attempts by untalented amateurs. Over the years, I've come to feel that most repairs should be left to competent gunsmiths. Even a thing as simple as the installation of sling swivels can ruin an expensive stock, if it's done wrong.

I'll have to admit, though, that finding a competent general gunsmith can be a problem, especially in some areas of the country. Slowly, over the last 30 years, gun repair has seemingly divided into two categories—the specialist, and the parts replacer. The specialist unquestionably rates the Gunsmith title. Another term for specialist might be custom gunsmith, and some of the things turned out by these people can be accurately described as works of art. Specialists, though, do not normally do routine repair jobs. Their work is relatively expensive, and there's usually a long waiting list. Also, many of them restrict their work to a particular brand or type of rifle or shotgun.

Local gunshops frequently employ parts replacers who are capable of installing a new factory replacement for a broken part. Many currently-made firearms have a generous tolerance allowance, and this helps the parts replacer, as the parts often require little or no hand-fitting. When the gun is older though, and no parts are routinely available, the parts replacer is usually not capable of making an entire new part from steel stock. For this, a real Gunsmith is needed. It should be noted, though, that over a period of time, parts replacers may develop gunsmithing skills.

The best guide a shooter or hunter can use in choosing a gunsmith is his reputation. Among the gun people in an area, everyone will know the inept practitioner as a "gun butcher." The reverse is also true, of course. A competent gunsmith will be known for his quality work. In instances where there is no clear recommendation, there is a way to check the skills of a gunsmith: Try him with a routine job on one of your ordinary pieces, before entrusting him with your fine Weatherby.

Any rifle or shotgun that has potential collector value is nearly always worth restoring to original working order. In the practical use category, though, a gun that is very badly worn might be beyond help. If the gun is an obsolete American piece or a foreign gun with no current importer, the cost of making replacement parts can easily exceed the repaired value of the gun. A gunsmith usually charges on the basis of his hours of shop time. This cost-may-exceed-value factor does not, of course, include the fact that the rifle or shotgun in question may have been used by the owner's father or grandfather. In that case, the customer may decide to have the work done, regardless of the cost.

Safety Rules

As I mentioned earlier, the original "Ten Commandments" of firearms safety still contain good advice for hunters and sport shooters, but they conflict occasionally with the concept of firearms used for personal protection. So, before we leave the Care Section of this book, I'll put down my own set of rules:

1. Watch the muzzle direction! (This is the equivalent of Rules 1, 4, and 6 in the original ten.)

2. Check to see whether the gun is loaded. Don't depend on the mechanism—visually inspect the chamber. Be aware that a round can sometimes "hide" in tubular-type magazines.

3. Never leave a loaded rifle or shotgun where it is accessible to children or inexperienced adults.

4. Be thoroughly familiar with all of the safety mechanisms of your shotgun or rifle.

5. When shooting, keep in mind the range and penetration possibilities. Be sure of your backstop. In home defense, remember that a wall will probably not stop a rifle bullet.

6. When shooting, be sure your companions are well to the rear of your firing point. Keep in mind that an ejected fired case from a semi-auto can cause an eye injury.

7. Be alert to the possibility of ricochet, from hard earth, rocks, or water. (It should be noted that bullets will ricochet from water only if fired at a very shallow angle.)

8. Carry your rifle or shotgun safely, in a case or with a sling.

9. Use only ammunition in a power range recommended for your particular rifle or shotgun.

10. Always remember that mechanical safety devices are no substitute for safe handling practices.

Section Two

Gun Cleaning

EVERYONE KNOWS how to clean a rifle or shotgun. You just open the action, and use a patch or brush with some solvent to swab out the chamber and bore. The operation described above is better than no cleaning at all, but there's a lot of residue that will be missed. A little further on, we'll look at some very thorough cleaning methods, applied to several types of rifles and shotguns. Right now, let's see if there are answers to several often-heard questions about firearms cleaning: Is there one best solvent? Is it better to use a brush, or a patch? Which type of cleaning rod is best, and which tip? Finally, is it harmful to the rifling if the cleaning is done from the muzzle end?

To the first question above, there is no answer, because there is no best solvent. Several good ones are available, and each is especially suited to a particular cleaning requirement. The same reasoning can be applied to patches, brushes, and cleaning rods. The one about cleaning from the muzzle, though, is not so easy to answer. With some rifles and shotguns,

cleaning from the muzzle is the only way it can be done. On the other hand, shooters of super-accurate benchrest rifles know that even the tiniest deformation or damage in the rifling at the edge of the muzzle can have a detrimental effect on accuracy. At first glance, this would seem to be another question with no answer, but it isn't.

The supposed hazards of cleaning from the muzzle have proved to be less certain than previously indicated. Using regular cleaning methods, even with a cleaning rod of hard material, there is not enough wear to be really significant. Of course, it would be possible to do the cleaning so carelessly and roughly that damage could be done to a rifling land at the edge of the muzzle. This could even be done during breech-end cleaning, if the operation was handled so roughly that the rod was actually bent. One way of preventing this sort of damage is elementary—just do every cleaning job with the same degree of care that should be used in all other aspects of handling firearms.

There is also a mechanical means of protect-

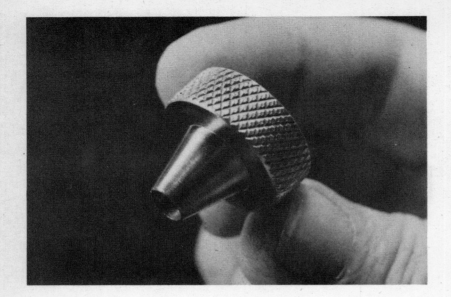

With some guns, cleaning from the muzzle is the only possible way. A muzzle protector will keep the rod centered, and prevent it from touching the rifling at the muzzle.

ing the rifling at the muzzle. It's known by several names, including "cleaning rod guide" and "muzzle guard." I've always used the latter term. Some of these are made to a particular bore size, but most are conical, so they can work in several calibers. They are usually of brass, nylon, or plastic, and they fit snugly on the cleaning rod. There is a knurled or ridged collar, so they can be held in the muzzle to center the rod, and keep it from touching the rifling. Some of the better cleaning rods come with muzzle guards, and they are also available as a separate accessory.

Cleaning rods are made of regular steel, stainless steel, aluminum, brass, fiberglass, nylon, and, in muzzle-loaders, of wood. Some of the metallic materials have also been used with a coating of soft plastic. When fiberglass was first used, it was mostly in the form of combination ramrod/cleaning rod units, for muzzle-loaders. Some shooters expressed concern about the possible abrasive qualities of fiberglass, and I did some tests on this. Using an ultra-sensitive Mitutoyo dial caliper from Brownells, I measured the inside diameter, land-to-land, of the rifling in an old section of cut-off barrel. I then ran a fiberglass rod through the bore a few thousand times. Finally, I used a piece of fiberglass

rod in an electic drill, and let it turn in the bore. The dial caliper was used again to check the land-to-land diameter, and there was no difference that could be measured. Apparently, fiberglass is not as abrasive as people thought.

Those who worry about such things have also expressed concern about cleaning rods that have a soft surface. The idea is that rods of fiberglass, nylon, aluminum, wood, or plastic-coated steel will pick up small bits of steel from the bore during normal cleaning, and that these imbedded slivers of steel will cut into the rifling. There is very small possibility of this, but only in certain circumstances. When the bore is not smoothly finished, it's possible that the edges of the lands might have some detachable steel slivers. If this is the case, using a soft rod could result in the conditions described. Then again, perhaps not. It has always been my feeling that the material of cleaning rods should be chosen for strength and solvent-resistance, and that any abrasive possibilities are so small that they are of no importance. I own and use cleaning rods made of all the materials mentioned, and many of the guns in which they are used are quite valuable. If I thought there was any chance of damage with certain materials, I wouldn't use rods of that type.

Equipment

Sectioned take-down cleaning rods are convenient for field use, as they can literally be made in pocket-size, if enough sections are used. I keep in the glove compartment of my truck a handy and low-priced rod kit called the Pac-Ram, made by Tipco Industries (87 Main Street, Hastings-on-Hudson, New York 10706). It has a knurled-end handle-piece and five aluminum 5¼-inch sections, and assembles into a 32-inch rod. The Pac-Ram kit is in a case of soft plastic

material here is solid brass, and the handle section has a ½-inch knob that is nicely knurled. Each of the five sections is 6 inches long. In the pockets of the soft plastic case are a slotted nylon patch tip, a mop, a bronze brush, and an accessory called a "bore obstruction tip," for pushing out any object lodged in the bore.

In the two kits just described, each made for a specific caliber range, a bronze brush is included. When a kit is made to be used for all

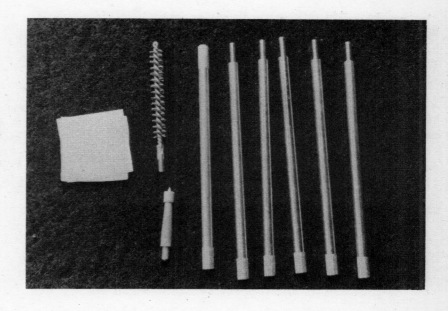

This aluminum sectioned rod by Tipco, called the Pac-Ram set, is pocket-sized, and assembles to 32-inch length. It is of good quality, and is inexpensively priced.

with separate pockets for each rod section, and a fold-in flap holds a bronze brush, a plastic patch jag tip, and patches.

In my range box is a similar kit, of higher quality and costing a bit more, by Outers (Box 39, Onalaska, Wisconsin 54650). Outers is one of the oldest and best names in cleaning equipment, and is now a division of Omark Industries (Box 856, Lewiston, Idaho 83501). The rod kit mentioned above is the Imperial Pak-Rod. The

types of rifles, shotguns and handguns, the brush is usually not included. Since brushes are made to fit certain bore sizes, the shooter should obtain brushes in the calibers he needs. Outers also has a small field cleaning kit called the Pocket-Pak, which has a "rod" that is actually a flexible steel cable sheathed in soft plastic. It's designed for pull-through operation. Included in this kit, which comes in a fold-over soft plastic case with a snap closure, are a bottle of Gun

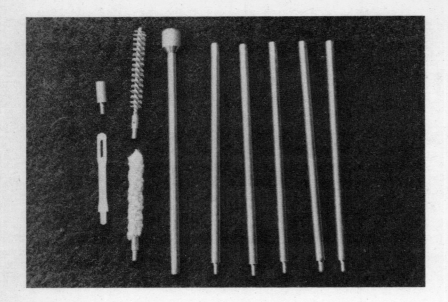

Made of high-quality solid brass, the Imperial Pak-Rod it by Outers features a nicely-knurled knob. It is available in different calibers, and includes a bronze brush.

The "rod" in the Outers Pocket-Pak Kit is a flexible plastic-covered steel cable. It also includes patch tips and brushes, patches, a gun cloth, and a bottle of Gun Oil/Solvent.

Oil/Solvent, patches, a silicone-treated cloth, two brushes, two patch tips, and an adapter.

For field use or the range box, the kits described above will do the job. For use at home, many prefer a more complete outfit. Outers has several of this type. Their Universal Kit will work for shotguns, rifles, and handguns, and comes in a hard plastic box with neat recesses for the items. There is a three-section free-turning aluminum rod with a large and comfortable

handle, the assembled length being 30½ inches. Also included are patch tips for rifle, shotgun, and handgun, knurled brush adapters, a box of patches, and bottles of Gun Oil and Solvent.

Another well-known and respected name in firearms cleaning equipment is Hoppe's, a division of Penguin Industries (Airport Industrial Mall, Coatesville, Pennsylvania 19320). They make a number of good cleaning kits, and one example is their Rifle and Shotgun Kit. It has a

Outers Universal kit has provisions for cleaning rifles, shotguns, and handguns, and the durable case is made of hard plastic for long wear.

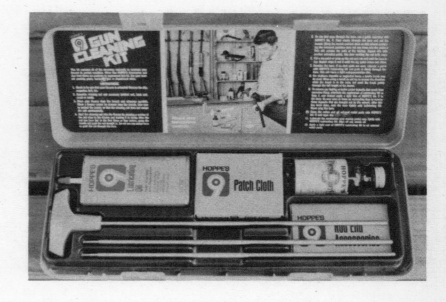

This kit from Hoppe's contains everything necessary to clean rifles and shotguns, including a bottle of the well-known Hoppe's No. 9 Solvent. The case is of hard plastic.

three-section brass rod that assembles to 32⅝ inches, one section having an attached free-turning handle. In compartments inside the orange hard plastic case are a can of Hoppe's Gun Oil, a bottle of Hoppe's Number Nine solvent, a box of patch material, and a box containing four different patch tips and four brushes, with an adapter. As a combination rifle/shotgun kit, it's excellent.

Outers offers a Rifle Cleaning Kit, in versions for specific caliber ranges. In a hard plastic box with recesses for the items are a three-section 30-inch aluminum rod with a free-turning handle, slotted and jag-type nylon tips, a bronze brush, Oil and Solvent, and a box of patches of the proper size. Also from Outers is a Deluxe Kit made especially for shotguns, with attachments for the three most popular gauges, 12, 20, and 410. In a hinge-top hard plastic box with a brass latch are compartments for a three-section

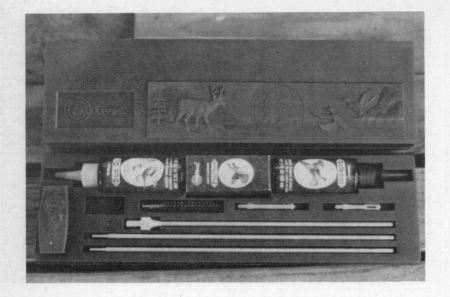

A separate rifle cleaning kit is available from Outers in versions for specific caliber ranges. In addition to the three-section aluminum rod and its accessories, it contains Gun Oil, Solvent, and patches.

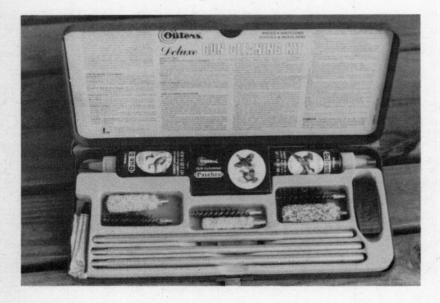

The Outers specialized kit for shotguns covers the most popular gauges, 12, 20, and 410, and also comes with oil, solvent, and patches, as well as a tube of Gunslick.

aluminum rod that assembles to 32¼ inches, two nylon slotted patch tips, and a pair of bronze brushes and mops for each gauge. Also included are bottles of Solvent and Gun Oil, a tube of Gunslick, and a box of patches.

For the blackpowder shooter, there is a kit from Outers that contains an extra-long four-section aluminum rod that assembles to 43 inches, enough for most muzzleloader barrels. For caplocks, there's a small plastic bottle with an attached soft plastic tube that fits on a standard nipple, to allow the solvent to be drawn into the bore by the suction of a patch. Two rod tips are included, a nylon slotted type and an aluminum jag tip. Also included are a box of cotton flannel patch material, and bottles of gun oil and blackpowder solvent. The case is the same as the one used with the shotgun kit described above.

All of these kits are fine for the hunter or

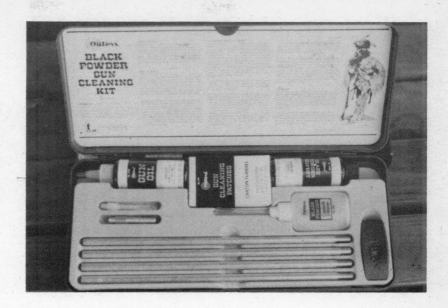

Outers has a kit for blackpowder shooters, and in addition to the regular cleaning accessories it also has a neat "caplock cleaner," a plastic bottle that attaches to the nipple and cycles the solvent through the bore.

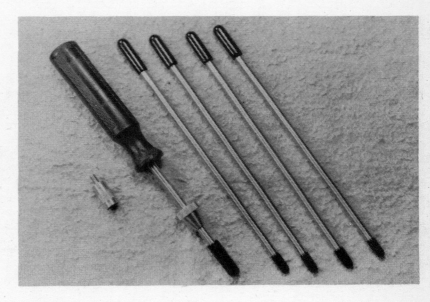

Among the separate rods, one of the best is the RIG-Rod, a sectioned stainless steel rod that is 31½ inches long when assembled. It comes with an adapter for shotgun accessories and a brass muzzle guard.

shooter who wants all of the necessary items in a convenient package. Some, though, prefer to assemble their own cleaning outfits, and for home use they will usually want a one-piece non-takedown cleaning rod. Before we look at some of those, though, there are two or three separate takedown-style rods that are not part of kits, and are too good to omit. One of the best is the RIG-Rod, by RIG Products, 87 Coney Island Road, Sparks, Nevada 89431. This fine stainless steel rod has a large plastic handle with a 3½-inch free-turning section, and four 7-inch sections, for a total length of 31½ inches. For convenient storage, all of the rod section ends are neatly capped in soft plastic. Included are a brass conical muzzle guard with a knurled collar, and an adapter for shotgun accessories. The endpiece will accept all standard cleaning accessories. This is a high-quality rod.

Beeman Precision Arms has long been known

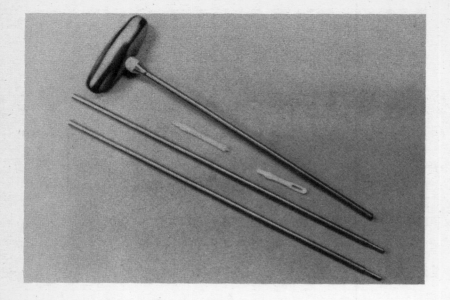

Long known for fine airguns, Beeman Precision Arms now offers firearms and cleaning accessories. One of the latter is a nice sectioned brass rod for 22 rifles that is 30 inches when assembled, and has an attractive striped-wood handle with a comfortable oval shape. The handle is free-turning, and jag-type and slotted tips are included.

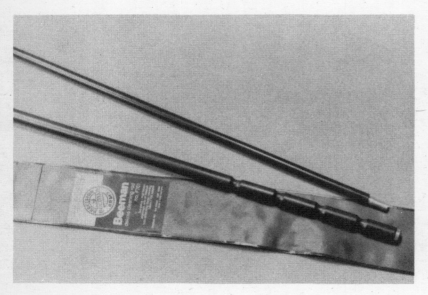

Also from Beeman is this two-sectioned shotgun rod, made in West Germany. It is of high-tensile aluminum covered in oil-resistant plastic, and assembles to 30 inches.

as a source for target-grade airguns, but in recent years this firm has added firearms and related equipment to its line, with an emphasis on high-quality and target-grade items. I have recently been trying a finely-made 22 caliber sectioned rod, 30 inches assembled, with a brass shaft and a comfortable handle of attractive striped wood. In the flap of its plastic case are pockets with a slotted and jag tip, both in nylon. The rod has a free-turning handle, and is very

well made. Also from Beeman (47 Paul Drive, San Rafael, California 94903) is a two-section shotgun cleaning rod, made for them in West Germany, that assembles to 36 inches, this measurement including the integral ridged handle. The rod is made of high-tensile aluminum, covered entirely in an oil-resistant plastic coating. In appearance, it resembles the takedown rods that are furnished with fine double shotguns. Its end is threaded to take an adapter that allows

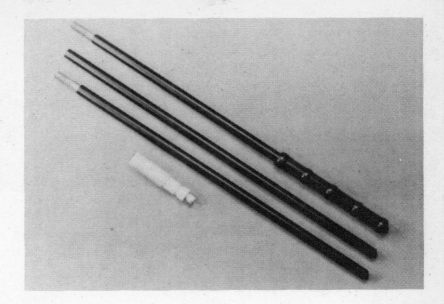

This Parker-Hale shotgun rod from England is imported by Freeland's, and has the same construction as the Beeman rod described above. It assembles to 36 inches, and comes with a combination jag/slotted tip.

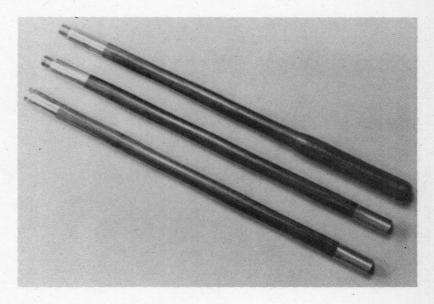

Dixie Gun Works offers a beautiful shotgun rod of rosewood with brass fittings that is in three sections, and is 33 inches assembled. It is very much like the ones that are usually supplied with fine English shotguns.

the use of all standard cleaning attachments.

While we're in the area of fine takedown-style shotgun rods, let's not overlook one made by Parker-Hale of Birmingham, England, and imported by Freeland's, 3737 14th Avenue, Rock Island, Illinois 61201. This is a three-section rod that is of similar construction to the Beeman's rod described above, plastic-sheathed aluminum with a ridged integral handle. It also assembles to 36 inches overall. Included with

the rod is a universal shotgun tip that is both slotted and a jag. This outfit clearly shows why Parker-Hale items are noted for their quality.

I have one other interesting take-down shotgun rod, and this one is from an unusual source —Dixie Gun Works (Union City, Tennessee 38261), the famous blackpowder supply house. This is a three-section rod, 33 inches assembled, and it is made of nicely-grained rosewood with fittings of solid brass. Included with the rod are

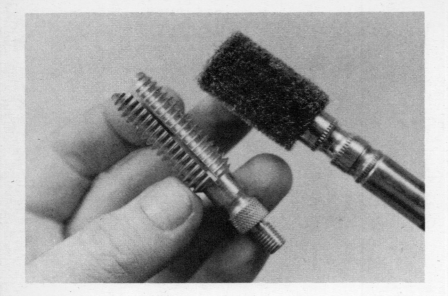

Included with the Dixie shot-gun rod are two accessories, a combination jag/slotted patch tip, and a very fine and dense brass brush. The quality of this rod and its tips is outstanding.

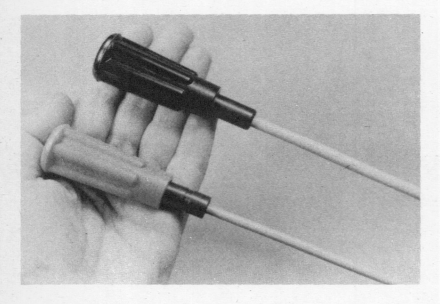

Two fine Parker-Hale one-piece rods from Freeland's. The 22 rod has a 40-inch shaft, and the larger one is 34 inches long. The steel shafts are plastic-covered, and the handles are free-turning.

two tips—a combination jag and slotted patch tip, and a brass brush with very fine and dense bristles. The workmanship of this rod and its accessories is outstanding, with very precise fitting and detailed knurling. It would look right at home in a case with a fine English double shotgun, and at the time this is written, it sells for just $37.50 plus shipping cost. The Dixie catalogue calls it "the finest rod of its type available today." I agree.

When storage space and portability are not factors, a one-piece cleaning rod is best. Sectioned rods, if used continually, will require occasional tightening of the sections. Also, if the rod is used frequently, and stored in its original box, it will have to be reassembled each time. Because of the absence of joining sections, one-piece rods tend to be a little stronger, less likely to kink. The handles of one-piece rods tend to be more comfortable and larger. The shapes

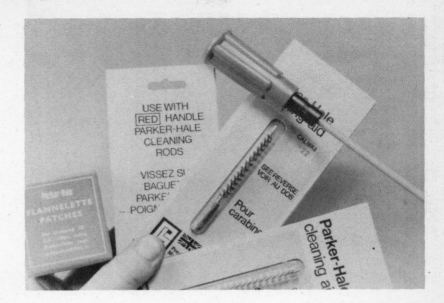

Parker-Hale rods will not accept standard cleaning accessories, but there is a wide assortment of Parker-Hale items designed especially for these high-quality rods.

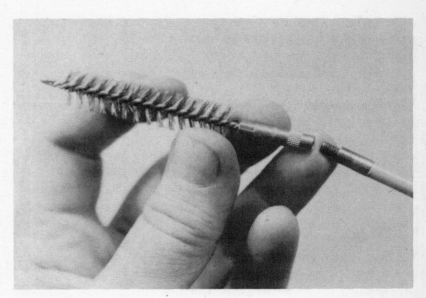

range from a round tear-drop shape with a guard flange to spherical, flat or onion-shaped knobs.

In the solid-shaft rods, let's look first at two made by Parker-Hale of England, and imported by Freeland's. My 40-inch rod is slim enough for 22 caliber, and the other, with a 34-inch shaft, has a diameter of .248-inch, to accomodate calibers from 270 upward. According to the Parker-Hale catalogue, these rods are coated in "acetate"—actually, some type of tough plastic. Under the coating, the rods are steel. The free-turning handles are ridged, screwdriver shaped and are comfortable to use. It should be noted that these superb rods will not accept standard attachments, as the male thread is on the rod. So, if you choose Parker-Hale rods, be sure to also get the special factory accessories.

I have two fine rods by RIG Products that are examples of exactly what a good cleaning rod should be. They are stainless steel, with free-

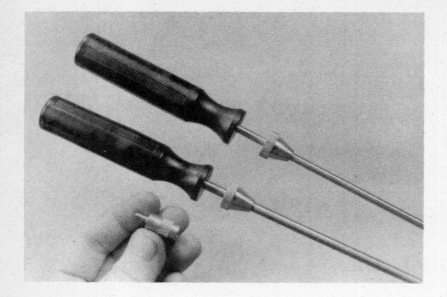

These two one-piece RIG-Rods are examples of what a good cleaning rod should be. The free-turning handles are perfectly shaped, both have integral muzzle-guards, and the shafts are stainless steel. The 22 rod is 30 inches long, and the larger one has a 36-inch shaft. With the larger rod, an adaptor for shotgun accessories is supplied.

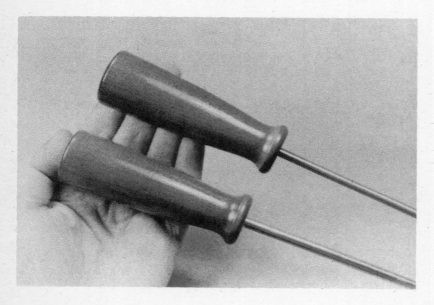

The Outers one-piece rods are also excellent, with large and comfortable hardwood handles and free-turning shafts, both 36 inches long. The smaller-diameter rod is of stainless steel, and the larger rod is brass. Both are, of course, internally threaded at the tips to take all of the many Outers cleaning attachments.

turning handles of black plastic that have a perfect shape. Both rods have conical brass muzzle guards with finely knurled collars, and soft plastic covers for the tips when they are not in use. The ends are threaded for standard attachments. One rod has a 30-inch shaft and is small enough for 22 caliber, and the other is 36 inches, of larger diameter, for 6mm and upward. I don't know whether the RIG people are actually manufacturing these rods or having them made, but

whoever is turning them out is doing a fine job.

The Outers Division of Omark Industries has a pair of excellent one-piece rods with large and comfortable free-turning hardwood handles, and both have 36-inch shafts. The smaller-diameter rod is stainless steel, and will handle 22 caliber and upward. The larger rod has a brass shaft, and it will work in any bore that is 30 caliber or larger. The tip of both rods is threaded internally to accept all Outers cleaning attachments, and

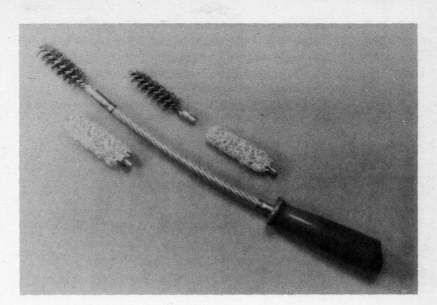

This Outers tool is designed specifically for cleaning shotgun chambers, and it comes with brushes and mops for 12 gauge and 20 gauge. The "shaft" is a plastic-covered flexible steel cable, and this allows it to be used on chambers without disassembly of the gun.

adapters are available to allow the use of some others. These are high-quality rods, and look as if they will last practically forever.

Outers also offers another interesting "rod," to use the term loosely, that is designed especially for cleaning shotgun chambers and gas systems. It comes in a kit that includes bronze brushes and mops for 12 gauge and 20 gauge, the two most popular chamberings. The rod has a handle that is identical to those on the rods described above, but without the free-turning feature. The shaft is a woven steel flexible cable, entirely sheathed in soft plastic. This allows the brushes and mops to be used on the chambers of semi-auto and slide-action shotguns through the ejection ports, without removal of the barrels. Thus, this tool can be used in the field or at the range, before the gun is taken home for cleaning.

As many readers will be aware, the old waxed-paper shotgun shells, when fired, left a film of wax in the chamber of the shotgun that actually served as a protective lubricant. Modern plastic shotshells are superior in many ways, including performance and resistance to moisture, but they do have one side-effect: They leave no lubricant in the chamber, and instead they deposit a heat-transferred plastic residue

that is slightly acid. In certain atmospheric conditions, this can cause a light coating of surface rust in the chamber in a very short time. So, brushing out and lubricating the chamber immediately after shooting is finished for the day is a good idea.

There is also another similar tool designed for this purpose, and it's also made in versions for rifles and automatic pistols. It's called Kwik-Kleen, and it has the advantage of being pocket-sized. In fact, the entire unit is contained in a neat plastic box that measures just 3¾ by 2¾ by 1⅛ inches. It consists of a 3-inch plastic handle, a 2½-inch flexible steel shaft, and a bronze brush and mop in whatever gauge or caliber is chosen. In operation, it works in the same way as the larger Outers unit described above. I have also examined a prototype military unit, finished in olive-drab color, which has a special combination bronze and stainless-steel brush that will clean both the chamber and the bolt-locking recess on an M-16 (or AR-15, or several other 223 rifles). For more information on these, the address is: Kwik-Kleen Company, Incorporated, Box 9764, Yakima, Washington 98909.

The cleaning rods we've covered here are not the only good ones, they're just a representative group of the types that are available. For most

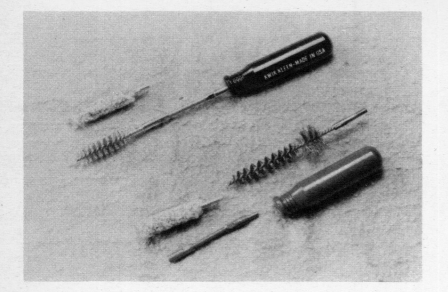

In a smaller, pocket-sized unit, the Kwik-Kleen tool is for the same purpose as the one described above. Shown below the regular Kwik-Kleen is a prototype of a tool developed for the military, to simultaneously clean the chamber and locking lug area of an M-16.

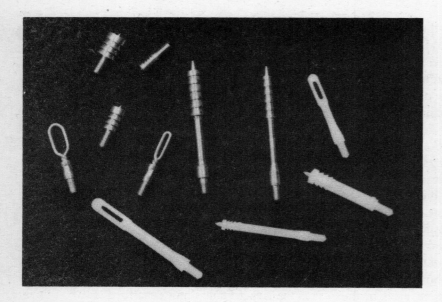

Here are several examples of jag-type and slotted patch tips for cleaning rods. Muzzle-loaders require that a jag-type be used, but otherwise it's a matter of personal choice.

of them, there are adapters offered that will allow the attachment of nearly all of the cleaning tools. Speaking of those, let's examine the rod accessories, and the way they are used. There are two basic types of patch tips—jag, and slotted. Jag types have many different shapes, but all of them have flanges or projections of some sort to grip a patch wrapped around the tip. Blackpowder shooters who use single-shot rifles and shotguns have to use this type, to reach the bottom of the bore and allow extraction of the patch. Many shooters of modern breech-loaders also like to use the jag tip, for its tighter fit in the bore, and for the convenience of just shaking a used patch off the tip.

The slotted tip also has its own advantages. It will keep the patch on the rod for repeated swabbing of the bore, and additional solvent can be added to the patch on the rod, if necessary. Actually, both types of patch tip do a good job,

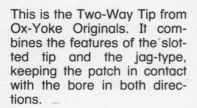

This is the Two-Way Tip from Ox-Yoke Originals. It combines the features of the slotted tip and the jag-type, keeping the patch in contact with the bore in both directions.

Along with the Two-Way Tip, the Ox-Yoke people also designed a special patch with "wings" that allow the material to lie back along the flutes of the jag in either direction.

so the individual shooter can choose the one that suits his purposes. A recently-introduced patch tip combines the features of both types. It's the Two-Way Tip, offered by Ox-Yoke Originals (130 Griffin Road, Suffield, Connecticut 06093). Made of brass, it has a slot at the center and jags at each end. The flanges angle toward the center, to hold the patch during both strokes, inward and outward. I've tried the Two-Way Tip, and it does a superior job. For use in this unique tip, Ox-Yoke also makes a special patch that is cut on each side almost to the center, making "wings" that lay back evenly on the jags, for better bore contact.

Traditionally, patch material is a soft flannel with one side rough and the other fuzzy. The preferred type of material seems to be pure cotton. For shooters who have the traditional approach, and who use a lot of patches, Brownells (Route Two, Box One, Montezuma, Iowa

The square patches are cotton flannel, from Brownells and Outers. The round ones on the right are from Hoppe's and are made of Reemay.

Here are some examples of mop attachments. They can be used for cleaning, but will soon be ruined. They are best used for preservatives.

50171) has excellent patches of pure cotton flannel, in bulk packs of 1,000, in four sizes. Patches in general are shaped round, square, or rectangular, and are sized according to caliber. Depending on the rod tip used, even a patch of the right size can fit too tightly in the bore. If this occurs, the simple remedy is to cut the patch smaller, until you arrive at a size that will be snug but move freely.

Generally, round patches work best with jag-type tips, and square or rectangular ones with slotted tips, but this is not necessarily a rule. Cotton flannel patches do a fine job, but there are good patches of other materials. Hoppe's offers patches of DuPont Reemay that have good bore-scrubbing properties. This material is made up of continuous-filament polyester fibers that are bonded together to form a lint-free material that has tiny loops and coils. These work to catch and hold particles of dirt and powder resi-

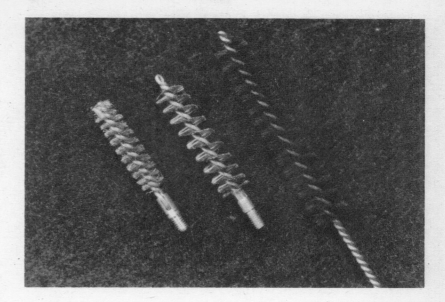

Brushes are made of nylon fiber, bronze, and stainless steel. The latter two are best.

due. There is also another advantage—solvents and oils are not absorbed by the material, they are held on the surface of the fabric for free application.

I have always reserved mop attachments for after cleaning, for the application of oil or some other preservative. They do a better job of this than a patch, because of their greater absorbency and long contact area. I'm not sure whether this was the original purpose of the mop, but I think it's the best use for them. While used patches are intended to be throw-away items, mops are not, and if they are used for primary cleaning, they will soon be ruined.

Bore brushes that are non-metallic used to have fiber bristles, but most of those made today are of nylon or some similar material. These are all right for the removal of loose powder grains or similar residue, but for hard scale or metal deposits, they are not effective. For these, you'll need a brush of bronze or stainless steel. A stainless steel brush will remove deposits even more effectively than one of bronze. In stainless steel, there is more spring to the bristles, and the brush will last longer than bronze. Bronze bristles eventually will become brittle and break off, or will "take a set" and lie down. Most of the makers of firearms brushes

now offer stainless steel, and in time, the bronze brush may be phased out.

The cylindrical brush is perfect for the bore and any other tunnel-like area of the gun, but it is almost useless for cleaning other parts of the mechanism. On any flat or convex surface, the round brush just doesn't have enough contact area. In these locations, a toothbrush shape is needed. Actually, a regular toothbrush is acceptable, if its bristles are fairly stiff and if you're brushing loose powder residue. Usually, though, toothbrushes that are used in gun cleaning are old ones, with worn bristles. A new one will work better, and a small-size child's brush is ideal, for getting into tight places. Something more substantial is needed, though, when you're removing powder scale, such as the baked-on residue on the front of a gas piston in a rifle or shotgun with this type of locking system. The brush that I use for this purpose comes from the Brownells catalog, where its stock number is 4D00PLL. It has a toothbrush shape, and its tied bristles are stainless steel. The sturdy handle is laminated wood. There is absolutely no better brush for the purpose, and I have kept one on my workbench for years. (No, not the same one —even this good brush will wear out, eventually.)

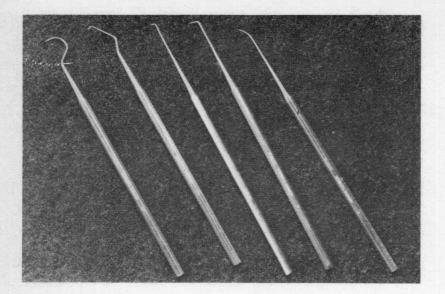

This set of dental tools has five shapes that are perfect for removing residue from tiny crevices. The tools are of stainless steel, and are available from Brownells.

Not even the best brushes will reach all of the areas in a rifle or shotgun that should be cleaned. The extractor and ejector recesses, for example, are places that can harbor a lot of residue. Narrow and deep spaces of this sort will usually require gentle scraping out with a small tool. A tiny screwdriver will do it, but the best implement of all is a dental tool. In their infinite variety of shapes there is one for every possible application, and they are made of stainless steel, with handles that are knurled. If your dentist can't supply you with some that he has phased out, Brownells offers a set of five useful shapes, and the cost is very reasonable. Their stock number is 2T00DES.

Most modern shotguns, whether slide-action, semi-auto, single-shot, or double-barrel, have barrels that are easily removable, so inspecting the bore is no problem. Just point the removed barrel toward a light source, and look through. Some shotguns and many rifles, though, don't share this feature, so checking the bore requires an accessory. There are devices that have angled mirrors, but these require a light source and a bit of maneuvering to get the right angle. Also, they give uneven illumination and blinding bright spots.

Most gun people now use what has come to be called a bore light. The minimum type is nothing more than an ordinary push-button pen-light with a Lucite endpiece that will bend the light into the chamber and bore. The most elaborate version of the bore light is one called the Conduct-A-Lite, marketed by Brownells. It has a nicely-turned aluminum body, and operates on two penlight batteries. It's number 7B10N87 in the Brownells catalog, and it comes as a kit in a soft plastic case, with accessories. In addition to the light, there's an extra short body for single-cell use, a spare bulb, three Lucite endpieces of different lengths and shapes, and a dental mirror that will clip onto the Lucite rods. You supply the batteries.

A bore light that I frequently use in my shop is the Flashette, a two-cell light made of tough ABS plastic, that uses a sub-miniature screw-in bulb. This light has a fixed extension arm that puts the light at just the right angle, and the translucent bulb cover gives a bright but soft non-glare light. Another advantage is a sliding switch on the side, so there's no need to hold down a button while you're using it. This is a well-engineered light, and it is very inexpensive. It's available from the Flashette Company, 4725 South Kolin Avenue, Chicago, Illinois 60632.

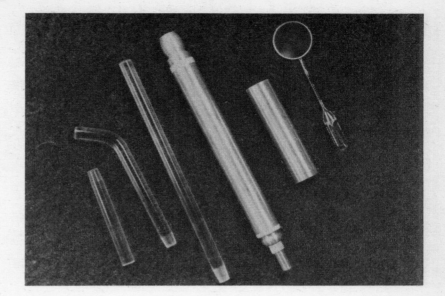

Brownells Conduct-A-Lite is a typical bore light, but is a more complete outfit, with three different Lucite extensions and a clip-on mirror.

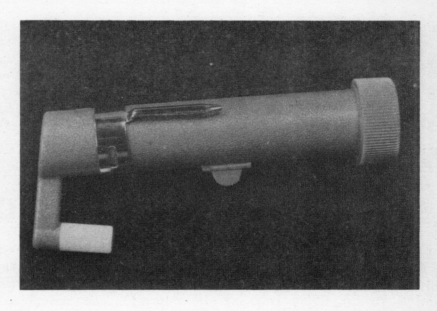

The Flashette is an excellent bore light of unusual design. Its translucent bulb cover gives a soft light in the bore, and it has a positive switch on the side. The case is of tough ABS plastic, and the fixed arm gives exactly the right angle to the light.

For a general view of the bore, the lights described above are fine. Sometimes, though, a lot of light may be needed in a particular place, or in some recess of the mechanism that's otherwise difficult to see. In that case, there's a perfect light available, and it's called the Probe-Lite. It's made by MDS Incorporated (Box 1441, Brandon, Florida 34299), and the initials in the company name stand for Medical Diagnostic Services. The Probe-Lite began as an item of medical equipment, and its extension, only $1/8$ of an inch in diameter, can be bent into any useful angle. The tiny bulb-end can even be inserted into a 22 caliber bore. This light has a positive toggle-type switch, and all components are replaceable.

In earlier years, there was really only one way to examine the bore of a muzzle-loading rifle, and that was to unscrew the breech plug. This was usually not an easy job, and it was not often

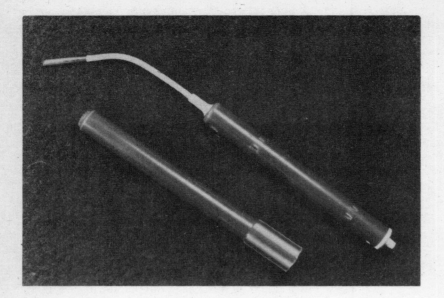

This MDS Probe-Lite is made by a manufacturer of medical tools, and it supplies an intense light. It has a tiny bulb, and its shaft can be bent into any shape. The switch is a positive toggle-type.

done, unless there was some other problem with the gun. Now, there is a way to look at the bore of a blackpowder rifle that takes only a few seconds, and no tools. Gremmel Enterprises (271 Sterling Drive, Eugene, Oregon 97404) imports an ingenious little light made by Lothar Walther of West Germany that makes possible a complete view of any bore that is .315-inch or larger. This light uses one of the tiny bulbs, frosted to prevent glare, that is attached to a steel weight. A 42-inch small flexible cord attaches to a two-battery (standard AA cells) case, and the miniature light is simply dropped down the barrel. It's inexpensive, and works perfectly.

Solvents and Lubricants

The twist of well-cut rifling or the mirror-polished bore of a shotgun are beautiful sights to anyone who appreciates fine firearms. It's not true, though, that a rough bore is inherently inaccurate. I have fired surplus military rifles with miserable bores that grouped amazingly well. In those cases, the bores were rough, but the rifling was still prominent. You might conclude from this that having a bright and smooth bore is not important, but this is not true.

If you fire cast lead bullets in a rough bore, you will soon have a serious leading problem, and this will begin to affect the accuracy. Even with jacketed bullets, there will still be an acceleration of copper-nickel deposits. These metallic deposits will occur, of course, even in a bore that is bright and smooth, and this is the reason for using solvents. For light deposits in a bore that is not pitted, just scrubbing with a stainless steel or bronze brush will remove some of the metal fouling, especially lead. As the brush exits the bore, you can actually see a shower of tiny lead flakes. Copper-nickel, though, will just be polished by the brush, and the only thing that will properly remove it is a good solvent.

The first one that most gun people think of is good old Hoppe's Number Nine. It does a fine job of loosening the lead and chemically breaking down the copper deposits, and it does this without harming the bore. One thing should be

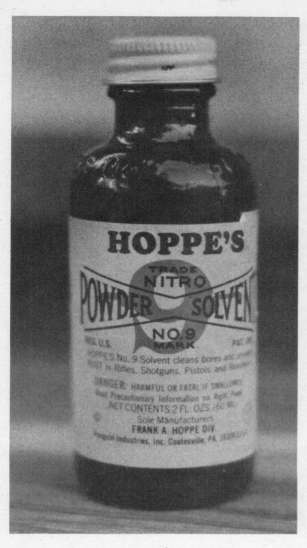

Hoppe's Number 9 has been around for many years, and is probably the most well-known of all bore solvents.

Very popular among target shooters is Marksmans Choice Number 7 bore solvent.

remembered, though, and this can apply to many other solvents: It should not be left in contact with plating, especially nickel. While few rifles or shotguns are nickel plated, some parts are—for example, the bolts of some 22 rifles. In the same way that the solvent breaks down the metal deposits in the bore, it can attack any plated surface, so keep this in mind. Hoppe's Number Nine comes in several forms: the familiar bottle, handy aerosol cans, and a 1-gal. drum.

Sinclair International, (1200 Asbury Drive, New Haven, Indiana 46774) markets several bore cleaning solutions, and these are well-known among benchrest and metallic silhouette shooters. Those who are active in these sports always strive for the smallest possible groups, so it makes sense to closely examine some of the items they use. Marksmans Choice bore cleaner is one of these, and it is very effective on copper deposits, lead, and powder residue.

Quicksilver is a cleaner that was made for use on small engines, but someone discovered that it also does a fine job on firearms.

The nickel plate caution applies here, and it will do harmful things to plastic and stock finishes. It is relatively expensive, but it works beautifully. Other specialized cleaners marketed by Sinclair include the Australian-made Sweet's 7.62 Solvent, specifically for copper removal, and Plumbex from West Germany, for the same purpose. Plumbex is a gel, and Sweet's is a liquid. I've heard good things about both of these, but haven't had occasion to try them. One Sinclair

item that I have used is Quicksilver, which is actually a cleaner for small engines. Someone discovered that it also works well as a powder solvent, and target shooters have been using it ever since. It will remove carbon from spark plugs in a running engine, so powder residue gives it no trouble at all.

Before we look at some other good solvents, I want to refer to a recent bulletin from Sinclair that contains some important information on "home-brewed" bore cleaners, often referred to among serious target shooters as "Blue Goop." The bulletin is headed "Bore Cleaning Caution," and I'll quote it here, in its entirety:

"For several years we've been using—and recommending the use by others—of "Blue Goop" on those barrels which are badly copper-fouled. However, a recent turn of events has caused us to pull in the reins and take a much closer look at the use of this home-brewed copper solvent.

"A customer from Louisiana called and told us that he had discovered pitting—easily visible with the naked eye—in the muzzles of three of his match grade stainless barrels. He reported using Blue Goop in the manner written up in *Precision Shooting* magazine, i. e., with the hydrogen peroxide added from the muzzle in a separate step. Interestingly, the accuracy of the rifles had seemingly not been harmed by the pitting in the muzzles.

"When the three barrels arrived at the shop to be shortened and recrowned, they were checked with a bore scope. The barrels were free of fouling and the pitting seemed to be confined to an area extending back somewhat less than an inch from the muzzles. After the barrels were shortened, the sections which were removed were cut in half for closer examination. The pitting was found to be both extensive and deep.

"To check things more carefully, a flat was milled on the outside of a stainless steel barrel stub. Three small depressions which would hold samples of cleaning solvents were milled into this flat. One of the depressions was filled with our own Blue Goop (which has hydrogen peroxide mixed in at the time it is made), the second with a mixture of 28% ammonia and hydrogen peroxide, and the third with stronger (28%) ammonia. The solutions were allowed to stand approximately 24 hours before the metal was checked for pitting. At the end of the test period, the section which contained 28% ammonia showed little or no pitting. The section which contained a mixture of 28% ammonia and hydrogen peroxide showed some pitting. The section which contained Blue Goop showed severe pitting. The test was repeated a second time with the same barrel stub, and the pitting became worse.

"At this point we would caution shooters who are planning to use either Blue Goop or any other cleaning solutions which rely heavily on stronger ammonia to be especially careful in the use of these solvents. If the solvents are left in the barrel long enough to evaporate, pitting of the bore surface is almost certain to result. While we can't be certain, it appears that the hydrogen peroxide mixed with the ammonia *may* be the culprit.

"This is not to say, however, that shooters should give up the use of these solvents entirely. We would recommend that the chamber be plugged with one of our chamber plugs, the bore filled *completely* with Blue Goop, and a piece of tape be put over the muzzle of the barrel to prevent evaporation of the solvent. Be certain to follow removal of the ammonia-heavy solvent with a careful cleaning and a liberal application of a rust-preventing oil."

While the concern in this interesting bulletin from Sinclair is barrel damage, it reminded me of the old time way of removing lead, which involved plugging up the barrel and filling it with mercury. Left for a time, the mercury would amalgamate with the lead, and the mixture was then just poured out. There are two good reasons why this method is no longer used: Mercury is a deadly poison that can be absorbed through the skin, and it is damnably expensive.

The chamber plugs mentioned in the Sinclair bulletin are precision-made of steel (12L14 screw machine stock) and are offered in ten different shapes and sizes, to fit chambers from 22 and 6mm PPC up to the belted magnums. I have number six, which fits 22–250 and 250 Savage,

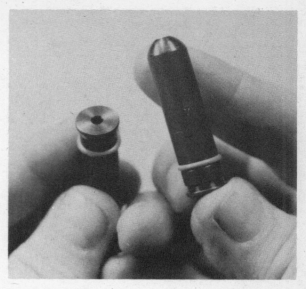

These Chamber Plugs, available from Sinclair International, are used to close off the lower end of the bore for treatment of the barrel with special copper solvents. They are made of steel, with a neoprene sealer ring, and come in ten sizes.

and number seven, which covers the 308, 243, and 7mm-08. The plugs are cartridge-shaped, with a rim that will function with the gun's extractor, and a groove on the body that holds a Viton seal ring, impervious to all solvents and lubricants. Even if you don't use the soaking routine described in the bulletin, these plugs are useful. Placed in the chambers of vertically-stored rifles, they will keep any solvent left in the bore from migrating into the action, or worse, onto the stock. The plugs are available from Sinclair for $7.90 each, plus postage.

Jim Brobst (299 Poplar Street, Hamburg, Pennsylvania 19526) has been making his popular "J-B" bore cleaning compound for more than 25 years. Many experienced shooters use it, but I hadn't tried it until very recently. It's a paste, and in this form it has some advantages over the liquid solvents. It is intended for use with patches only, and is extremely effective for removing powder residue and metal deposits. A property that Jim stresses is that it's "non-em-

J-B Bore Cleaning Compound is a non-imbedding paste that is very effective in removing deposits of copper and lead from the bore.

This Nitro Solvent by Birchwood Casey is available in several forms, including the regular liquid shown.

bedding,'' meaning that it can be cleaned out of the bore easily with just a dry patch. Since it is a compound, its elements will tend to separate over a period of time, so it should be stirred before use. J-B Compound is inexpensive, and works well.

Among many other fine products for gun care, the Birchwood Casey division of Birchwood Laboratories (7900 Fuller Road, Eden Prairie, Minnesota 55344) makes a fine Nitro Powder Solvent that also contains a rust inhibitor. I use it often for general action cleaning. Outers has an excellent Nitro Solvent that does a fine job of removing powder residue and copper deposits. One of its ingredients is acetone, so care must be taken to keep it off wood finish. It will also react with some plastics, so keep this in mind if your gun has any parts of this material. This doesn't mean you shouldn't use it, just keep any large quantity from staying in contact with any plastic parts. Outers Nitro Solvent is offered in liquid and in spray cans. The Jet-Aer Corporation (100 Sixth Avenue, Paterson, New Jersey 07524) has G96 Nitro Solvent, and one

of its important properties is an ingredient that neutralizes the acid residue that plastic shotshells leave in a shotgun chamber.

There are many good solvents—I've just covered a few examples here. Several of them are offered in both liquid form and in aerosol spray cans, and some of the latter have a slim plastic tube that attaches to the spray button, allowing very precise application. There are two advantages in having the solvent in spray form,

Outers Nitro Solvent comes in both aerosol and regular liquid form, and a combination Solvent/Oil mixture is included in several of the cleaning kits offered by Outers.

A special ingredient in G96 Nitro Solvent by Jet-Aer removes the plastic residue left in shotgun chambers by modern shells.

the most obvious being that it can be directly sprayed into inaccessible areas of the mechanism. The aerosols also avoid the slight loss of volatile ingredients from evaporation that can occur with liquids. And, the spray solvent is easier to apply to patches and brushes. I have seen shooters dip cleaning brushes directly into solvent bottles, but after this is done a few times, the solvent solution is fouled and loses some of its effectiveness.

With its metal deposits, the bore demands a solvent, but in other areas of the gun, there is another type of cleaner that will actually work better, especially when there is excess oil and a lot of residue. These cleaners are classified as de-greasers, and one of their uses is as a pre-treatment chemical in cold-blue kits. I have a small spray can of Jet-Aer G96 Spray Gun De-Greaser that was part of such a kit. The main use of these cleaning solutions, though, is gen-

One of the uses of this G96 de-greaser is the removal of oil from steel surfaces to prepare them for cold bluing, but it also works as a cleaner.

Birchwood Casey Gun Scrubber is one of the best-known of the de-greasers. I use it often.

eral removal of residue and oil from actions, and I use them very frequently. On the workbench right now I have Birchwood Casey Gun Scrubber, Outers Crud Cutter, and RIG 3.

The de-greasers are all in aerosol cans, and most have the small insert tube for precise application. Most have as an ingredient 1,1,1-trichloroethane and other halogenated solvents, so they should always be used with adequate ventilation, preferably outdoors. Also, avoid extensive skin contact. With the proper care, though, they are quite safe, and they evaporate quickly, leaving a clean and dry surface. There is nothing else that will do this job as well.

Shooters of muzzle-loading rifles and shotguns know that blackpowder cleaning calls for special solvents and operations that are perhaps more thorough than those used on modern smokeless-powder guns. If the residue from blackpowder is left in the bore and on other surfaces, it will quickly form corrosive salts that can ruin a gun overnight. The old-fashioned way of cleaning was with soap and hot water, and this will definitely work. The modern solvents, though, will do it better and more easily, as their chemicals are more efficient at breaking down the residue.

Crud Cutter is the picturesque name of the Outers de-greaser. It does an excellent job.

A recently-introduced de-greaser is RIG 3. Like the other chemicals of this type, it efficiently removes all traces of residue and oil, and quickly evaporates.

Many of the manufacturers of regular firearms cleaning solvents also offer products especially designed for blackpowder use. There are also a few solutions that are made in smaller quantity, and offered by suppliers of other muzzle-loading items. For 10 years, I had a magazine column called "The Powder Horn," which last appeared in *Gun World* magazine, so I had an opportunity to test all of them. All will do the job, some more quickly than others. It should be pointed out that my use of some of the products mentioned goes back to the beginning of my magazine column, so it's possible that some of these may not still be available.

Two of the blackpowder cleaning solutions that I've used are concentrates, designed to be mixed with a specified quantity of water. One of these is Black-Solve, made by the Chopie Man-

Buffalo Spit and Black-Solve, two good black-powder solvents, are in concentrated form, and are mixed with water before use.

Like several of the other blackpowder solvents, Thompson/Center Number Thirteen can be used as both a patch lubricant and a cleaner.

ufacturing Company, Inc., 531 Copeland Avenue, La Crosse, Wisconsin 54601. A small bottle makes a quart of cleaner when mixed with water. The other concentrated solvent is called Buffalo Spit, and this one is offered by Fort Greene Ville Trading Company, 2 Front Drive, Little Hocking, Ohio 45742. It's supplied in a 16-ounce bottle with about 1½ inches of solution in the bottom, and you just fill the bottle with water, and mix the solution.

Quite a few of the blackpowder solvents also double as patch lubricants, so in effect you "clean as you shoot." While this may sound strange, it does work, because it reduces the amount of fouling and makes it easier to load the following shots. Because of this use, many blackpowder solvents come in soft plastic bottles with flip-up applicator spouts, and one is even in a bottle shaped like a powder horn.

Well-known for their fine blackpowder rifles,

Hodgdon Powder Company separates their blackpowder solvent and patch lubricant, the solvent being called Spit Bath, and the lubricant Spit Ball.

The combination blackpowder solvent and patch lubricant from Hoppe's is called Hoppe's 9 Plus. It works as well on blackpowder as the old No. 9 does on smokeless residue.

Thompson/Center Arms (Box 2426, Farmingdale Road, Rochester, New Hampshire 03867) has a solvent called Number Thirteen that also serves as a patch lubricant. The Hodgdon Powder Company separates its solvent and patch lube into Spit Bath and Spit Patch, respectively. The Hoppe's blackpowder solvent is Hoppe's 9 Plus. At Birchwood Casey, it's Number 77 Black Powder Solvent, and this one also is used by many non-muzzle-loading target shooters.

There's really no reason against using any of the blackpowder solvents to clean cartridge rifles or shotguns, but they often do not have the metal-deposit removers of nitro solvent solutions.

Totally Dependable Products (Box 277, Zieglerville, Pennsylvania 19492) has a fine blackpowder solvent that I have used frequently. It's called TDP SS 1, and it comes in a 5-ounce aerosol can with an applicator tube. It is unusual among the solvents because it is harmless to

Birchwood Casey Number 77 is a popular black-powder solvent, but it is also used by many target shooters, according to the people at the Sinclair Company.

I have always found that the items made by Totally Dependable Products live up to the company name. The TDP blackpowder solvent is called SS I.

wood, rubber, painted surfaces, and most of the plastics. In addition to this, it will not stain most fabrics, yet it does a good job on blackpowder fouling. I've found that all of the TDP products live up to their name—"totally dependable."

I'm not sure whether it's still being made, but at one time the J. M. Bucheimer Company (Box 280, Frederick, Maryland 21702), better known for quality leather goods, also offered a Cleaner and Patch Lubricant that had penetrant proper-

ties. At their suggestion, I once sprayed it in the bore and on the external surfaces of a blackpowder gun after firing, and waited several days before cleaning it. There was no rust. Still, it's best to clean immediately after the day's shooting.

Jet-Aer offers a G96-brand Black Powder Solvent and Patch Lubricant, also in an aerosol can, and it has penetrant and metal fouling action. All of the G96 products work just as their

At one time, the Bucheimer Company, known for fine leather goods, made a good blackpowder cleaner and patch lubricant. I'm not sure whether it's still available.

G96 Blackpowder Solvent and Patch Lubricant, made by Jet-Aer, works well.

labels indicate. The last two solvents mentioned have a penetrant content, and I think this ingredient needs some additional comment. Perhaps the best-known of the penetrant solutions is WD-40, and when it's used for its intended purpose, to loosen parts that are stuck by rust, it does a marvelous job. However, it is not an efficient preservative. My friend Ken Davis inherited a Remington Model 870 shotgun, and since he did not intend to use it right away, he stored it in a dry closet in his home. Unfortunately, he made two errors. He sprayed it liberally with WD-40, and zipped it into a vinyl case. When it was taken out after several months in the closet, there were areas of surface rust on the barrel and receiver. What could have gone wrong?

The very qualities that make penetrants like WD-40 do such a fine job on rusted parts require a "thin-ness" that keeps them from being an efficient protective coating. In the case of

WD-40 and SS P are fine penetrants, but they don't offer long-term surface protection.

Ken's gun, there was the added factor of a closed vinyl case, trapping any ambient moisture and keeping it in contact with the steel of the receiver and barrel. There was probably high humidity on the day the gun was put away. Even with these factors, though, the gun would not have rusted if it had been coated with RIG, or some other good preservative.

In my shop, when I need a penetrant, the one I often use is SS P, made by Totally Dependable Products. It has freed a lot of rust-frozen parts, including the solidly-stuck action of a Stevens Favorite rifle that had been in a fire. I have also used SS P in many non-gun applications. Several times, a single squirt on the rotor shafts of non-running electric motors has restored them to operation. A caution, though, about all penetrants: In firearms use, be sure they are not left in the mechanism in locations where they could migrate onto cartridges. Their super-penetrating action can kill primers. If the rifle or shotgun is being used in defensive mode, a misfire could be the last thing you remember.

One item that I always keep in or near my gun cabinet is a treated gun cloth, to wipe down the rifles and shotguns a final time as they are put away. In the far past, I just used a piece of soft flannel that had been sprayed with a good preservative. Now, there are commercially-made treated cloths, impregnated with lubricants and other protectants, often with silicone. Outers offers a 17-inch square of pure Canton flannel, silicone treated, that can even be washed without harming its properties. The cloth from Birchwood Casey is about 15 inches square, and it is also silicone-treated. From the same maker is a small Sheath disposable cloth in a pocket tear-pack, handy to carry in the field.

I don't know the ingredients of the treated cloth from Hoppe's, but its texture suggests silicone. They also have a small disposable cloth, theirs treated with MDL (Moisture Displacing Lubricant). From RIG Products is an oval pad of real sheepskin with lubricant and silicone, called a RIG-Rag, an inelegant name for a high-quality item. All of these cloths are good to have around for the times when a full surface-treatment isn't called for, but a quick wipe-down might prevent an ugly fingerprint rust-mark.

While we're on the subject of treated cloths, there are two special-purpose types I want to mention. One is the Wipe Away, made by Belltown, Ltd., Route 37, Box 74, Sherman, Connecticut 06784. Actually, this cloth is mostly used on handguns, specifically on revolvers. When lead spray accumulates on the cylinder

Shown here are examples of gun cloths impregnated with protective elements, offered by RIG, Outers, Hoppe's, G96, and Birchwood Casey.

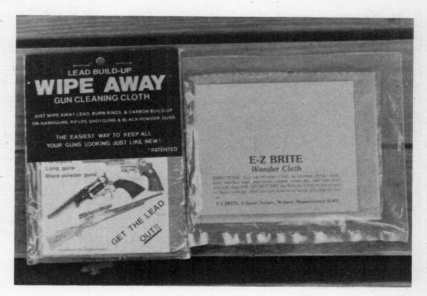

Two special-purpose cloths: The Wipe Away will remove lead spray marks from the muzzle, and in patch-cut form will remove it from the bore. The E-Z Brite cloth can't be used on blue, but is great for brightening brass furniture on muzzle-loaders.

face, this cloth will simply wipe it away. However, it also has application on rifles and shotguns, as it can be cut into patch size and used to do its wipe away thing in the bore. Its ingredients are a secret, but whatever is in it, it works. It sells for just $4.95.

The first thing to remember about the E-Z Brite Wonder Cloth is that it must *never* be used on blued steel, as it will neatly remove this finish. On stainless steel or nickel plate, though, it will just remove lead and carbon deposits. It also does a superb job on brass, and is an easy way to bring back the shine to brass furniture on muzzle-loaders. Over the mantlepiece in the living room I have a nice little Euroarms flintlock carbine, and when I checked it recently, its guard and other brass fittings had turned quite dull. After a minimum amount of rubbing with the E-Z Brite, it looked almost like new. This cloth is available for about $3 from the E-Z

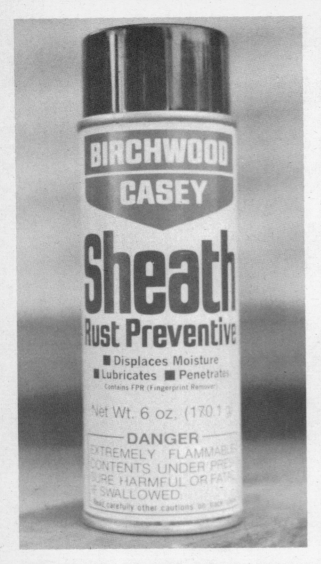

Sheath, by Birchwood Casey, is well-known as an effective protectant.

Beeman Precision Firearms offers this fine lubricant and protectant, MP-5 Oil.

Brite Company, 6 Susan Terrace, Woburn, Massachusetts 01801. And remember—*don't use it on blue!*

When a shotgun or rifle has been cleaned well, there are still two elements of gun care to be considered: The external finish must be protected, and the internal mechanism must be lubricated, both for protection and smooth operation. There are many good external preservatives, and while they may have some differences in chemical composition, their function is similar. Some are also lubricants, and some have wax, grease, or moisture-displacement ingredients. In choosing a protectant, you should consider the conditions under which the gun will be used, and try to fit the preservative to the conditions.

Sheath, by Birchwood Casey, is a combination protective coating and lubricant, polarized to cling to metal. It also has an ingredient that

From Totally Dependable Products, SS 2 and SS 2 Plus are excellent protectant/lubricant solutions.

In the lubricating and protecting area, Hoppe's has MDL, a rust inhibitor, and Dri-Lube, which contains Teflon.

neutralizes perspiration acid from fingerprints and removes them. It comes in liquid and in aerosol cans, and it is not harmful to the finish on stocks, nor will it harm plastics or rubber. MP-5 Oil, from Beeman Precision Firearms (47 Paul Drive, San Rafael, California 94903), has practically identical properties, and is a non-aerosol liquid. The MP in its designation stands for Metalophilic, meaning that it has polarized molecules that will seek the surface of metal,

displacing any moisture. Beeman has a reputation for handling only high-quality items, so this oil is worth trying on that basis alone.

There are two aerosol protectants from Totally Dependable Products, called SS2 All-Purpose Gun Lubricant and SS2 Lubricant Plus. These are excellent lubricants and protectants, and each comes with an applicator tube; they also have penetrant properties. This is especially true of the Lubricant Plus, which also has a mois-

A Teflon-content protectant from Outers is Tri-Lube (formerly TR-3), and they also offer an aerosol Gun Oil.

Moly Dri is a new "dry" lube from RIG. I use their other lubricant/protectant, RIG 2, frequently.

ture-displacing ingredient. Neither of these will harm wood, painted surfaces, rubber or plastics. It should be noted, though, that some of the protective solutions—and most of the solvents—can cause spotting on some plastic surfaces, such as the acrylic finish on some shotgun stocks.

Two dual-purpose protective lubricants are offered by Hoppe's in aerosol cans. There's MDL, the initials meaning "Moisture Displac-

ing Lubricant," and its action is fairly self-explanatory. The other one is Dri-Lube, and it contains DuPont Teflon. The liquid spray will evaporate in just a few seconds, and it leaves behind a dry surface that guards while reducing friction. It contains no stickly oils or silicones. The Teflon is in suspension, so to insure even distribution the can must be shaken between each application.

Outers also has a pair of different preserva-

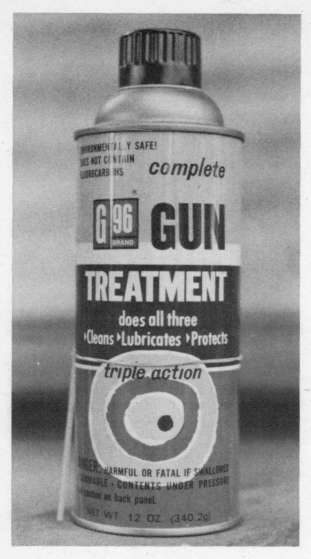

G96 has an all-purpose lubricant and protectant that they call Complete Gun Treatment.

so you should be cautious about stock finish and plastic parts.

At one time or another, I have used all of the items covered here, and they all work well. It's not my intention to endorse any one product. However, I'll have to admit that I have used RIG products for many years, especially the original grease. In more recent times, I have been using their RIG-2, a dual-purpose lubricant/protectant that is a combination of corrosion inhibitors, acid neutralizers, oils, and waxes, along with a moisture displacer. The other protectant from RIG is called Moly Dri, its main ingredient being MoS_2 that leaves a quick-drying film of non-oily lubricant. Moly Dri is particularly suited for semi-auto rifles and shotguns, especially those with gas operation, in which oil is not a good choice of lubricant.

It just occurred to me that the last sentence above might not be understood by readers who are not familiar with gas-operated guns. In shotguns and rifles having this type of locking system, all of the components of the gas system must be kept clean and *dry*. If any oil-type lubricant is left on these areas, the heat of the ported gases will quickly bake it into a hard scale that is not easy to get off. Also, if there is excessive build-up of this scale, it can even retard the movement of the components, and the gun will stop functioning. Here is a good general rule for all gas-operated guns: No oil-type lubricants forward of the receiver.

Break-Free CLP, made by the San-Bar Corporation (9999 Muirlands Boulevard, Irvine, California 92714) would have been an appropriate inclusion in any of the already-covered categories, as it will do nearly everything. The CLP in the name means "Cleaner/Lubricant/Preservative," and it will do all of these. Its ingredients have a neutral PH factor (neither acid nor caustic), and it easily removes powder residue. Its properties of lubrication are particularly good, and it keeps its action at extremes of temperature. Under laboratory conditions, it prevented rust and corrosion in a humidity chamber for more than 900 hours, and it with-

tives. One is an aerosol can with a tube applicator that has a very simple label: Gun Oil. This is designed to be used inside and outside, and as it is actually an oil, it has superior lubricating properties. It is also offered in non-aerosol bottles, as a liquid. Really better for external treatment is Outers Tri-Lube. It has Teflon, a penetrant, and a lubricant, and gives long-lasting protection to the surface. Like some of the solvents, Tri-Lube contains 1,1,1-trichloroethane,

The nearest to an all-around solution for gun lubrication and protection, Break Free CLP has passed some impressive laboratory tests, and is used by the military.

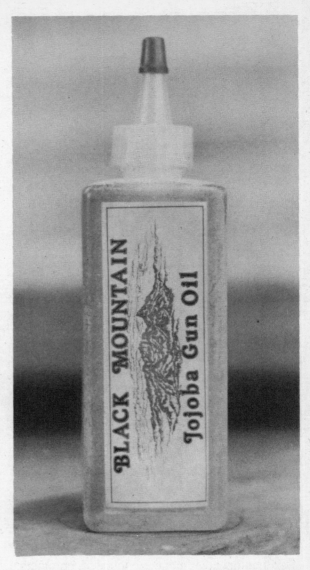

Jojoba Oil has amazing properties. It's a perfect chemical substitute for sperm oil.

stood more than 100 hours in a 5 percent salt spray. There are penetrant properties, but they are not so pronounced that it will migrate and cause primer damage. (It is, of course, always a good idea to keep any type of lubricant away from cartridges.) Though Break-Free will lubricate on application, its effect will improve after is has ''cured'' for a few hours. It is used extensively by the police, the military, and by competition shooters.

In earlier days, if you asked an experienced hunter or shooter what he considered to be the perfect lubricant, his answer would likely have been sperm whale oil. Its properties included high adhesion to metal surfaces, resistance to extremes of pressure and temperature, and anti-corrosive action. It was obtainable, unfortunately, from only one source, and the sperm whale is now a protected species. Sperm oil is not rountinely available, and when it can be found,

Here are two excellent lubricants that were developed especially for use on stainless steel: CS Lubricant, and RIG +P.

it is damnably expensive. And, it does have some minus points: It will not keep well, and it has an aroma that is less than pleasant.

There is, however, an oil that has all of the chemical properties of sperm oil, and none of its disadvantages. It comes from a plant that grows in the southwestern United States, *Simmondsia chinensis*. Popularly called the Jojoba (that's pronounced ho-HO-bah), it has been known for a long time as an ornamental shrub and browse plant. More recently, it has begun to be cultivated for the beans it bears, which can be processed into a waxy oil. Jojoba oil never turns rancid, even with long storage, and it is odorless.

For blackpowder shooters, Jojoba Oil is an excellent patch lubricant. When used as an internal lubricant, it is long-lasting and adheres well to the parts. As a protective coating, its wax properties impart a surface that is non-sticky and resists fingerprinting. Also, it works just as well on stock wood, and on slings and other leather items. It's amazing stuff, and I hope it's still available (I haven't seen it lately). It was marketed as Black Mountain Jojoba Oil, and the address on my one remaining bottle is: Tri-M Ranches, Route One, Box 539, Ramona, California 92065.

The first firearms use of stainless steel was in handguns, but now there are several rifles and at least one shotgun made of this material. One of the early problems with stainless was galling, a transfer of metal from one surface to another in areas of pivoting or sliding parts contact. The stainless guns of today have almost entirely eliminated this by making the mating parts of differing stainless alloys, but stainless still has surface properties that differ from regular steel, and this has resulted in the development of special lubricants. One that I've used for several years is CS Lubricant, by CS Laboratories. 4219 South Walhaven Court, Las Vegas, Nevada 89103. It has a rather strange consistency, somewhere between a grease and a cream, and it's light blue in color. It has particularly good adherence to parts, and will not migrate to other areas. Though it was designed especially for stainless steel, it also works well in regular steel actions, and I use it often for lubrication of hammer and sear engagements.

RIG Products recently introduced a special lubricant in this category. It's called RIG +P Stainless Steel Lube, and it is a dark brown color, a grease-like preparation that is used in the same way as the one just described. Though I haven't yet used it to the extent that I have CS Lubricant, it also works well in both stainless and non-stain-

Left—on any rifle or shotgun that is being put away for long storage, an application of RIG Universal will insure that there will be no rust.

Above, right—Formula 15 Gunwax is a good protectant for both metal and wood. On collector pieces that are handled with some frequency, it will prevent fingerprints.

less guns. With the performances of other RIG products in mind, I'm sure it will prove to be fine for long-term use.

No discussion of protectants would be complete without the inclusion of RIG Universal Grease. Actually, the name contains a redundancy, because the acronym RIG originally translated to "Rust Inhibiting Grease." About 10 years ago, in my magazine column, "The Gunsmith," a reader who had a problem with surface rust on stored guns asked me what I used for this purpose. I said, truthfully, that I always used RIG. Well, at that time, RIG was not a regular advertiser in that magazine, and several other makers of protectants *were*. To say that they were less than pleased with my answer would be an understatement. Before this re-telling results in another stack of icily formal letters from the other manufacturers, let me quickly add that there are a number of excellent preservatives, and they are described in detail in this book. Also, I will admit that RIG has one disadvantage. It is a grease, and when it is applied to the surfaces of a rifle or shotgun, that gun will be greasy to the touch. On the guns that I use frequently, I use several of the other products mentioned. When a gun is being put away for a long period of time, though, I still use RIG. It's the best protection that is available.

Most gun collectors like to show their pieces,

and some that I know will even let people handle them, if they're sincerely interested and careful. There is, however, always the chance that a fingerprint will go unnoticed until later, even if the gun is wiped down afterward. On the faint blue of an early Parker double, a salty fingerprint can cause rust in a fairly short time. For display and handling, a non-greasy protectant is needed. A product I have just tried may be the answer for this. It's called Formula 15 Gunwax, and it's made by Frontier Products Company, 164 East Longview Avenue, Columbus, Ohio 43202. It is a combination of silicones and Carnauba wax, and it's used in the same manner as the other waxes that are used on furniture or shoes. Not only does it protect against fingerprints, but it also gives some protection against scratches. It can be used on both the metal and the wood, and you can leave it in a dull finish, as applied, or you can buff it to a rich shine. It works just as its maker claims, and it's inexpensive.

Another wax-based product that I've tried is Rust Guardit, an aerosol spray that deposits an even protective film on all surfaces. It has good holding power, and it dries to the touch in 30 seconds. It won't crack, peel, evaporate, or cake, and does not attract dust or dirt. When you want it off, it isn't difficult to remove (any good solvent will do it). In laboratory tests, it prevented rust and corrosion in salt spray for 48 hours, and in 100 percent humidity at 100 degrees for 30 days. A 10-ounce can costs around $4, and it will do what they say.

Cleaning Methods

The ways of cleaning a rifle or shotgun can vary widely, from just running a patch or brush through the bore to detail-stripping and washing the parts in a pan of solvent. Usually, the latter treatment is done only by gunsmiths, when a gun is about to be refinished, or in cases of guns that have been dropped into water. A complete-takedown cleaning once or twice a year is a good idea, especially if the gun sees a lot of use, or if it is carried in a rack in a pickup truck, in a dusty environment.

Among some of the "good ol' boys" in my part of the country, it's a fortunate gun that even gets carried in a rack. More often, it's tossed into the space behind the seat, along with tools, tow-ropes, and mud boots. One of the few 22 semi-auto rifles that will keep working under these conditions is the Remington Nylon 66, but even its legendary reliability can be affected if the dirt gets too deep. Just before writing this, I examined a Nylon 66 that had entirely stopped functioning. A takedown showed nothing mechanically wrong, and after a large quantity of dirt and powder residue was removed from its action, it worked perfectly. The people at the gun shop know the owner of this gun well, and they say we'll see it again, right after hunting season.

The case described above is not unusual. Quite a few of the rifles and shotguns that are brought in to the gunsmith for repair are not broken—they just need to be thoroughly cleaned. This is especially true of semi-autos, but it can apply to any type of action. Rifles in 22 caliber rimfire are particularly susceptible, partly because of the wax-like lubricant used on many 22 rimfire cartridges. It combines with flakes of unburned powder, oil, and dust to make a gum-my residue that routine cleaning seldom completely removes. If there is enough build-up of this stuff, parts of the mechanism will be affected.

While this problem is often seen in 22 rimfire rifles, centerfires and shotguns are not immune to it. I've seen an Ithaca Model 37, the most mechanically efficient slide action shotgun ever made, completely stopped by an accumulation of residue. The owner of that one, who used it year-around for skeet, trap, and hunting, and never cleaned it, couldn't figure out why it no longer worked. Just as with the rifle described above, a complete disassembly and thorough cleaning restored it to perfect operation.

This sort of thing couldn't happen with a blackpowder rifle or shotgun, because the cleaning rules are much more strict. Any muzzle-loader left uncleaned, even for a day, will be quickly ruined. After shooting, the gun must be thoroughly cleaned before the acid residue of blackpowder can begin to eat away at the metal surfaces. The fouling in the bore builds up rapidly, and during extensive shooting shooters usually "run a patch" between groups. If this is not done, loading will become increasingly difficult, and accuracy can be affected.

My own cleaning methods for all types of shotguns and rifles usually fall somewhere between the gunsmith's complete disassembly and the minimum of a quick brush through the bore. If your methods are not exactly like mine, this doesn't mean you're doing it wrong. If the system you use removes all of the glop, then keep doing it. Some who are reading this, though, may be just beginning in the shooting sports. For them, the methods described and shown on the following pages may be helpful.

Rifles

In centerfire rifles, routine cleaning usually involves a minimum amount of takedown. Since a tight fit of the action in the stock affects accuracy, separating them is normally done only in extreme cases, such as immersion in water. With bolt action centerfires, the usual procedure is just to remove the bolt, and, if it has an external floorplate, the magazine system. The 22 rimfires, whatever the action type, usually are taken down further, separating the stock and action. Lever action rifles often require some minor gunsmithing for removal of the bolt, so they are frequently cleaned by just opening the action. The factory manuals that are supplied with new rifles always contain some instructions for cleaning-takedown. If the manual is not with your gun, there are books that have this information—for example, my Firearms Assembly/Disassembly series, available from DBI Books. Here are my methods for cleaning rifles:

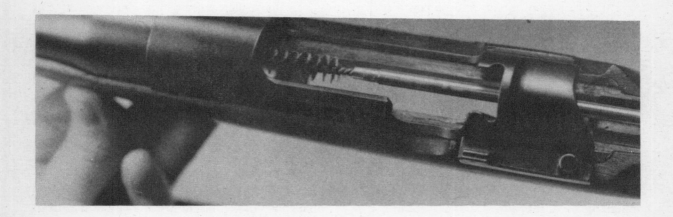

1. (Above) First, use a dry bronze or stainless steel brush of the proper size to brush out the bore. Work from the chamber toward the muzzle, if possible. If you prefer, this can be done with a non-metallic brush and solvent, but I prefer to first brush out any loose residue.

2. (Right) Be sure that the entire brush exits the bore before you draw it back through. If the brush is a tight fit in the bore, as it should be, the laid-back bristles will otherwise make it difficult to reverse. If the barrel steel is soft, as it is in many 22 rifles, an in-bore reversal of the brush may even cause rifling damage.

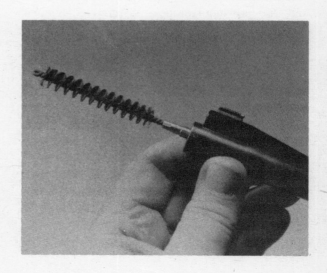

3. The chamber is always very slightly larger than the bore, and a properly-sized bore brush won't do a good job of cleaning the chamber. Whenever it's possible, I use a brush of the next size upward to brush out the chamber. The Kwik-Kleen unit is shown here, but a regular cleaning rod can also be used for this purpose. A turning motion should be used.

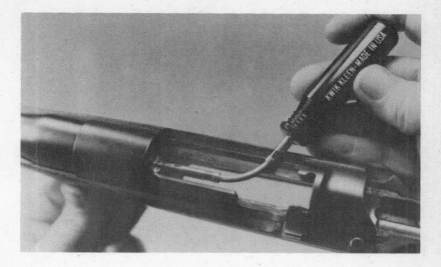

4. (Right) When a slotted patch tip is used, the patch can be put through the slot and dipped into the solvent bottle, but it shouldn't be re-dipped after a run-through, or the solution will be contaminated. If an aerosol solvent is used, it can be applied as shown.

5. (Below) When the saturated patch enters the bore, some of the solvent will be squeezed out, so take care that an excessive amount doesn't run into the action— or, if cleaning from the muzzle, onto the stock. Keep a cloth handy to absorb any excess.

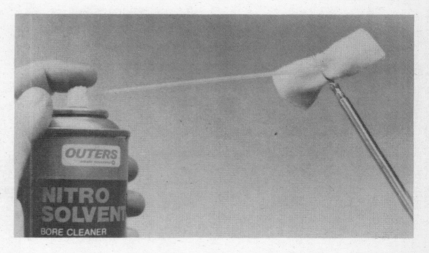

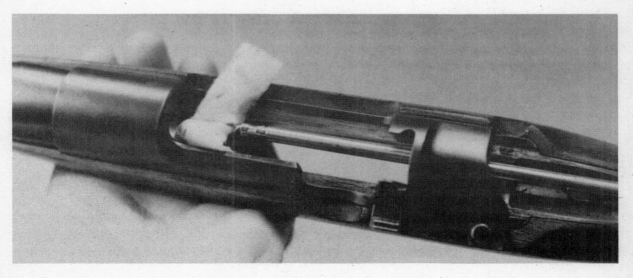

6. When the tip and the patch appear at the other end, stop before it exits the bore and reverse the stroke. Repeat the run-through several times, keeping the patch in the bore.

7. (Below) In rifles that have a box-type magazine, brush out the magazine well. This is especially important in 22 rimfires, as powder flakes and other residue can accumulate here.

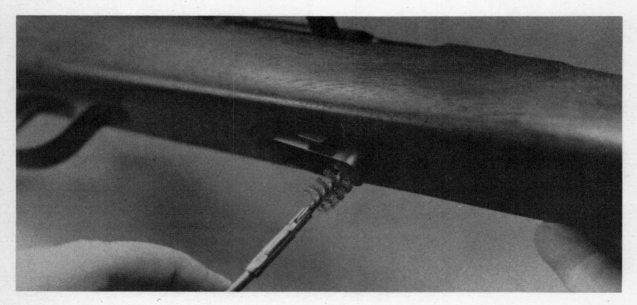

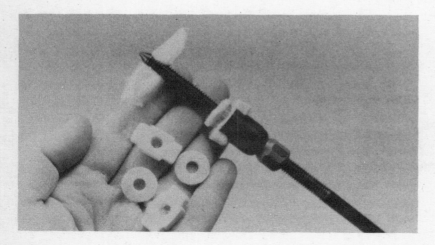

8. (Left) For bolt action centerfires, Brownells offers this cleaning tool that not only gets the chamber, but also has replaceable "felts" that clean out the bolt lug recesses, an area usually overlooked.

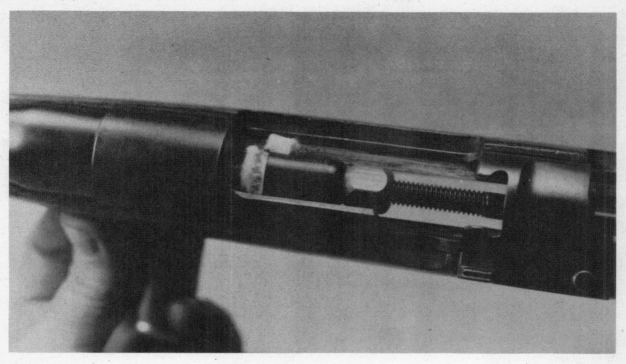

9. (Above) In use, the tool is simply inserted into the receiver and turned, with the solvent-saturated patch and the felts doing the job. This is an ingenious and useful tool, and it costs just $12.50.

10. (Below) Using the Brownells stainless steel brush or any other suitable implement, clean the face of the bolt.

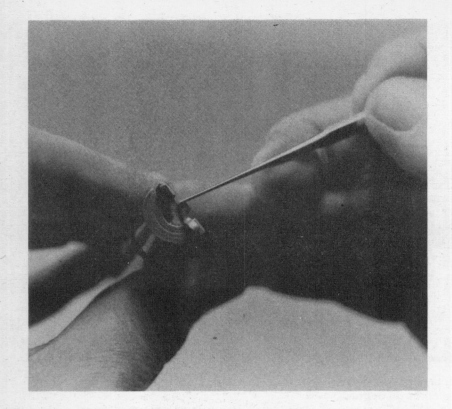

11. Be sure that any residue is removed from beneath the beak of the extractor. In cases of extreme build-up, it may be necessary to remove the extractor, to clean out its slot in the bolt.

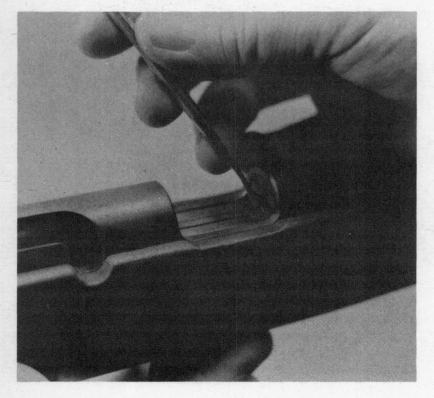

12. Another area in which residue accumulation can interfere with proper operation is the extractor recess at the edge of the chamber. Use a small screwdriver or a dental tool, as shown, to clean it out.

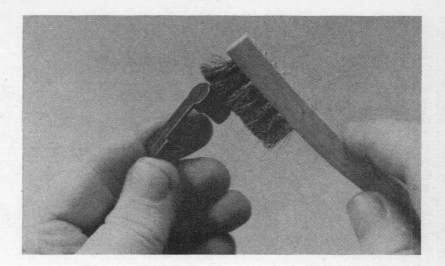

13. In 22 rimfire rifles, especially semi-autos, the magazine often gets quite a lot of residue, and most of those made currently can be taken apart. Here the follower, the platform that lifts the cartridges, is shown being cleaned.

14. (Above) Use a bore brush of appropriate size to clean out the inside of the magazine body. This can also be done with a patch and some solvent.

15. (Right) Any flakes of unburned powder that enter the magazine will drift down to the inside of the floorplate, so be sure to brush it off before the magazine is reassembled.

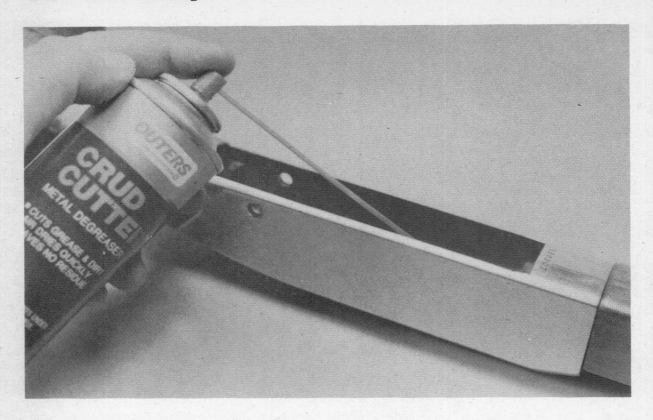

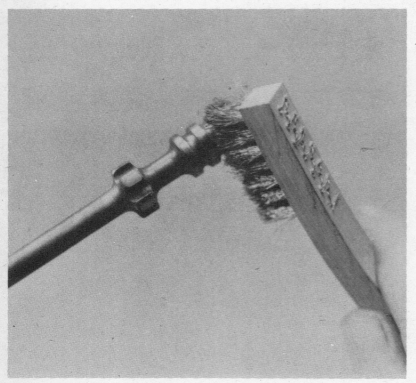

16. (Above) Certain ledges and recesses on the inside of the receiver may have to be individually brushed or scraped, but a good general job can be done by using a de-greaser, such as Outers Crud Cutter. Be sure to do this over some sort of receptacle, or outdoors, as the solution will run freely out of the receiver.

17. (Left) In gas-operated rifles, like the Galil shown, use a stainless-steel brush to clean the powder film from the surfaces of the gas piston and its tube.

18. (Above) After the piston is cleaned, use a bore brush of appropriate size to clean out the gas chamber. A 28-gauge shotgun brush is perfect for this, on the Galil.

19. (Right) When the cleaning is finished, a preservative can be applied to the bore by saturating a patch and making one pass through the bore.

20. (Left) For preservative application, a mop attachment is even better, as it will give more uniform distribution.

21. (Below) When the protectant-saturated mop is inserted into the bore, a portion of the solution will be squeezed out, so do this over a spread newspaper. I usually just hold a shop cloth at the entry point, then use it later for a wipe-down of the exterior.

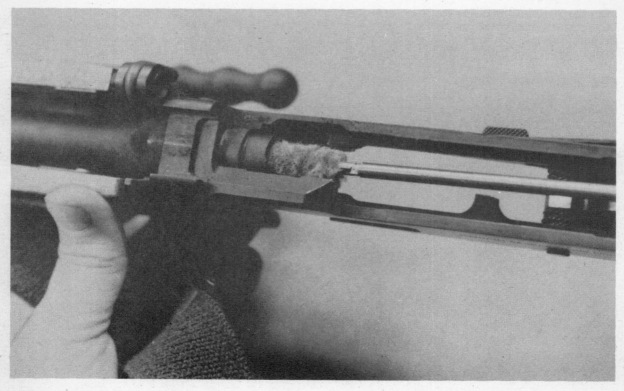

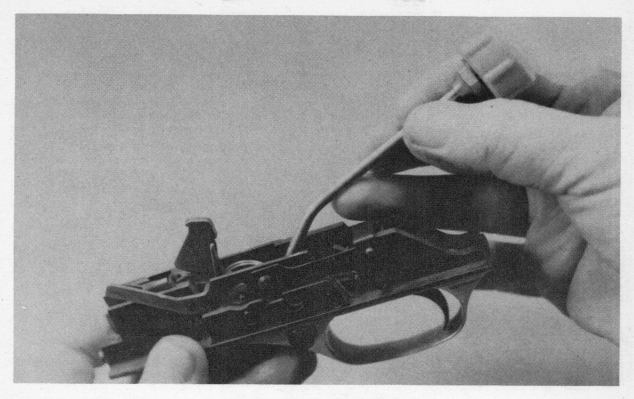

22. (Above) Oiling of the internal parts should be done very sparingly, just a drop or two on parts at their pivot point. Here, a drop is being applied to the sear and hammer engagement.

23. (Below) A light oiling of the bolt will smooth its action, but take care not to apply too much. Excess oil can combine with firing residue to make a gummy substance that can retard parts movement.

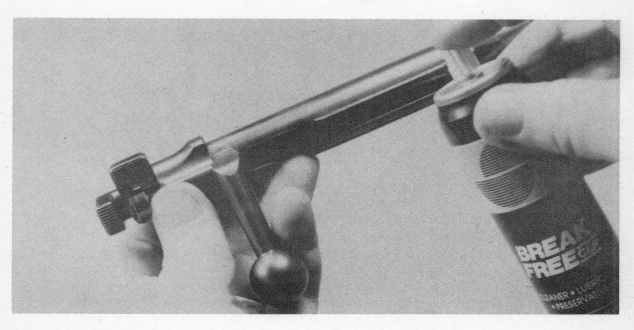

24. If the preservative you use is harmless to stock finish, it can be sprayed on as shown. My usual method is to spray a small amount in various locations on the metal surfaces, then spread it with a fingertip.

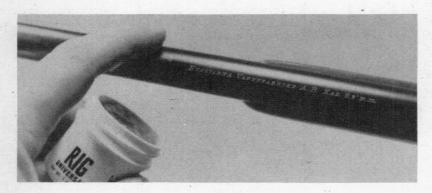

25. If the gun is not to be used again soon, or is a collector piece being put away, the preservative that I use is RIG. This can be done with a cloth, but I usually use a fingertip.

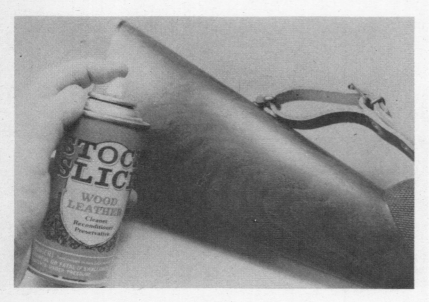

26. The wood of the stock will also benefit from the application of a surface protectant, and there are several good ones available. Shown here is Stock Slick, by TDP, which also works well on slings and other leather items.

Shotguns

From the standpoint of cleaning, shotgunners have an advantage over rifle shooters, in that most modern shotguns are easily dismountable. Barrels can usually be removed by just turning a knurled cap, and trigger groups can be dropped out of the receiver by pushing out one or two cross-pins. Even in older guns, such as the Winchester Model 12, takedown is not difficult. Shotguns have been made in every action style used in rifles, but the lever action was phased out early, and is now seen only on collector pieces. Bolt actions are popular because of their low price, but I won't show them here, as their cleaning procedure is the same as the one used for bolt action rifles. There are several cleaning operations, though, that are peculiar to shotguns, especially the slide-actions and semi-autos. Here are my methods:

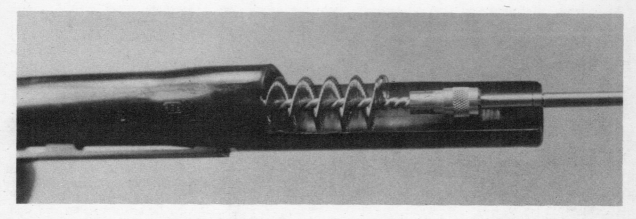

1. (Above) With a dry bronze or stainless steel brush of the right size, brush out the bore. Shown is the new Hoppe's Tornado brush, a springy spiral of stainless steel that contacts every portion of the bore with a stiff but smooth edge. Non-metallic brushes and solvent can also be used.

2. (Right) Allow the entire brush to leave the bore before reversing the stroke to draw it back through. When the brush is a tight fit, reversal in the bore can cause the laid-back bristles to dig in, and in the softer steel of shotgun barrels, this can cause scratching.

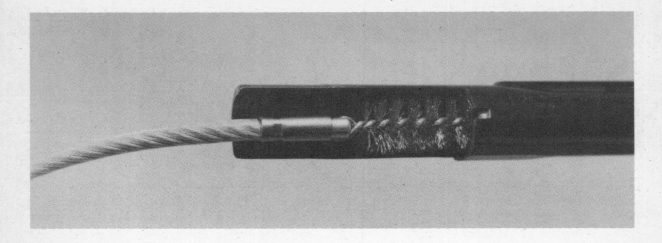

3. (Above) Use a brush of slightly larger size to clean the chamber. If you have it, the Outers tool shown will do a fine job. Use a turning motion.

4. (Left) If a jag-type tip is used, the patch can be wet by folding it over and holding it on the solvent bottle, or it can be saturated at the chamber edge if a spray solvent is used.

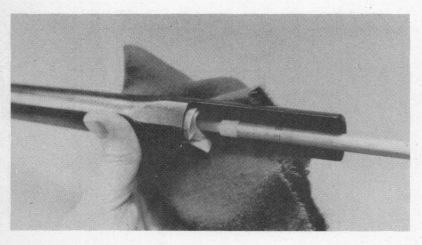

5. When the wet patch is started into the bore, some of the solvent will be squeezed out, so hold a shop cloth to catch the excess, or spread a newspaper.

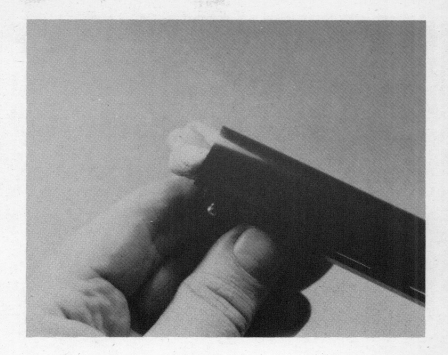

6. When the patch and tip are just visible at the other end of the bore, reverse the stroke and draw it back through. Keeping the patch in the bore, repeat this several times.

7. (Below) If it's not a major gunsmithing job to do it, remove the trigger group. The carrier (or lifter) will often accumulate residue, so clean it off thoroughly.

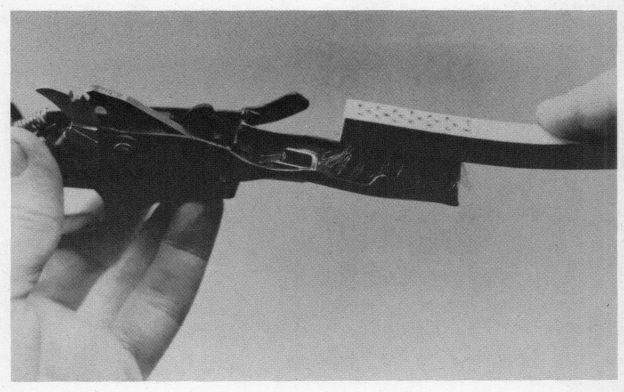

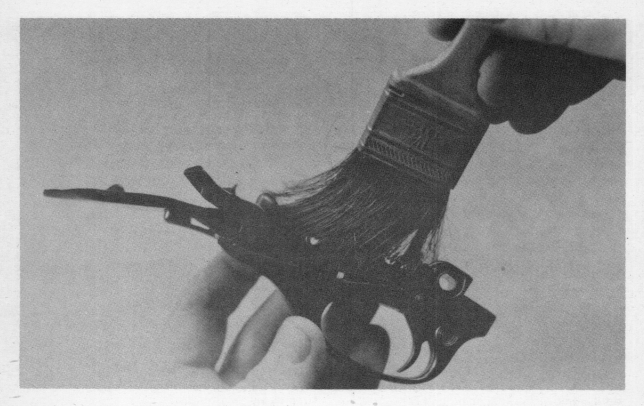

8. (Above) Unless the build-up of residue is severe, the rest of the trigger group mechanism can often be cleaned by using a dry soft brush, such as the paintbrush shown. When there is oily residue, use a spray de-greaser.

9. (Below) Inside the receiver, use a spray de-greaser to flush out residue. Do this outdoors, or over a suitable container, as the solution will run out freely. Some of the recesses and ledges inside the receiver may require scraping or brushing.

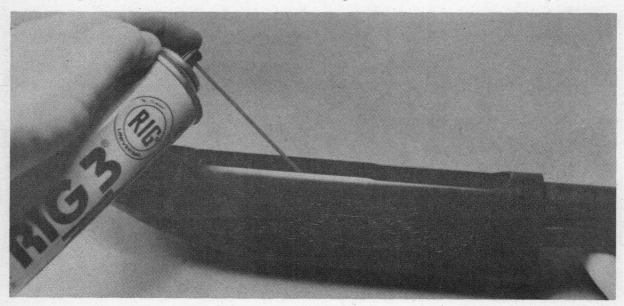

10. (Right) Clean any residue from the face of the bolt. I use the Brownells stainless steel brush for this, but it can be done with any brush or a cloth, and solvent can be used.

11. (Below) The ejector groove on the bolt is another area that can accumulate residue. Use a small screwdriver to scrape it out.

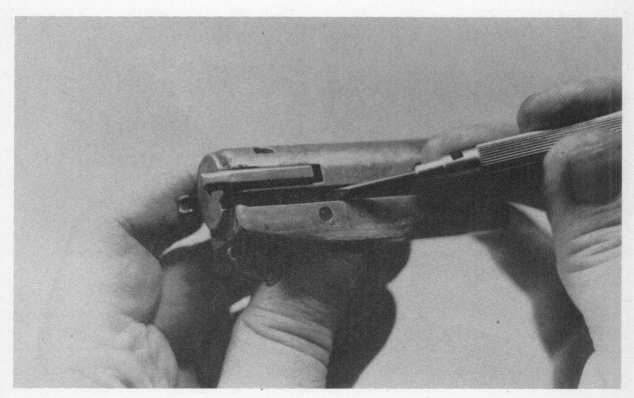

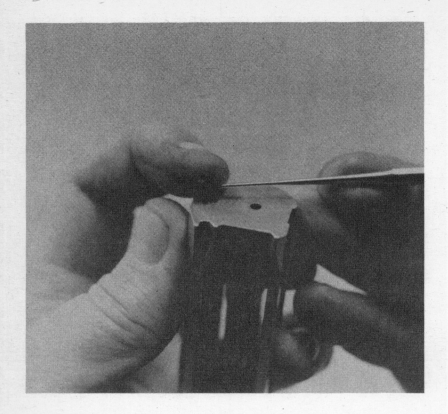

12. (Left) If residue builds up on the underside of the extractor beak, it can interfere with extraction. When dirt gets into the extractor channel, it will be necessary to remove the extractor for proper cleaning.

13. (Below) When the extractor has a separate recess beside the chamber, be sure it is cleared of any residue that might prevent proper extractor contact with the rim of the shell.

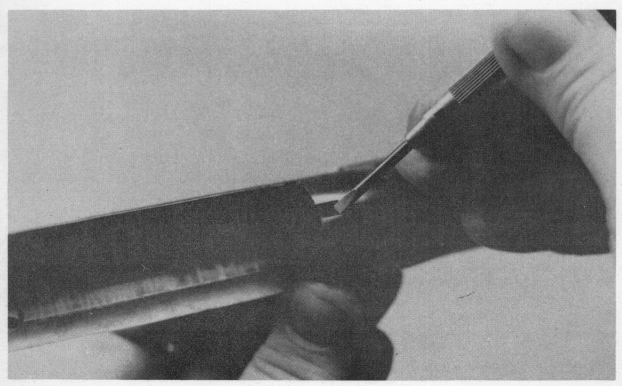

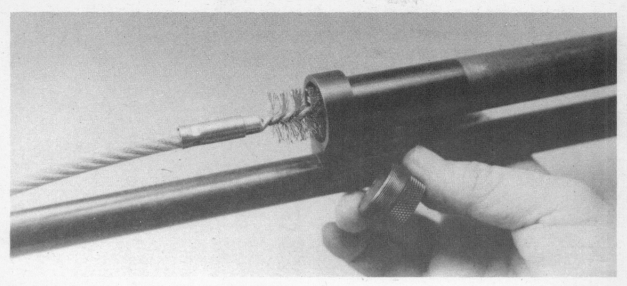

14. (Above) Most shotgunners are familiar with the removal of the magazine components, from installation of the limiting plugs required for hunting certain game. With retainer, spring, and follower removed, clean inside of the magazine. Since it is somewhat larger than the bore, use next size of brush, or improvise a larger patch from cloth.

15. (Below) When the shotgun is gas-operated, use a stainless steel brush to remove powder film from surfaces of the gas piston.

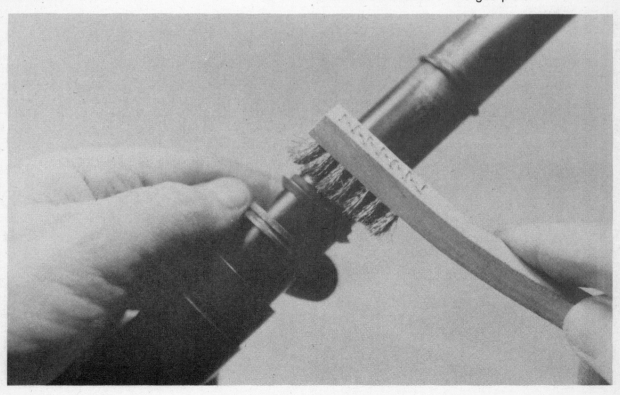

16. (Above) In most cases, the gas chamber is so large that there is no suitably-sized brush. A good job can be done, though, by using the Brownells stainless brush in a circular motion.

17. (Below) If there is build-up that constricts the gas ports in the barrel, they can be cleared with a pipe cleaner treated with a de-greaser. For this purpose, the best ones to use are the Ream-N-Klean bristle-type, made by Bryn Mawr Smokers Sundries, Inc., 3256 North Halsted Street, Chicago, Illinois 60657.

18. (Above) If your gun is equipped with an adjustable choke device, use a stainless steel brush to remove the powder film from its vanes and interior.

19. (Below) After cleaning, apply a protectant to the bore. This can be done with a patch, and a single pass-through and return will do it.

20. (Above) A mop attachment is better for applying preservative, because its density distributes the solution more evenly. Use a cloth to catch any excess.

21. (Below) Use oil very sparingly, just a drop or two at the pivot point of parts, and at the engagement of the hammer with the sear.

22. (Above) The bolt and its components can be lightly oiled to smooth the action, but don't over-do it. Also, if the gun is gas-operated, remember: Do not use oil on any part of the gas system. It should be left clean, and dry.

23. (Below) When applying external preservatives, I usually put a small amount on the metal in various locations and spread it with a fingertip. If you are using a protectant that is harmless to the finish of the stock wood, then it can just be sprayed on.

24. (Left) For guns that are to be put away until the next hunting season, an alternative to grease is a wax, such as the Formula 15 Gunwax shown here. It can be applied with a fingertip or a cloth.

25. (Below) For internal lubrication of stainless steel guns, such as the Snake Charmer 410 shown, there are specialized lubricants like CS and RIG +P. They are applied in the same locations as described for oiling. Just as with oil, only a small amount is necessary. These grease-like substances can also be used on guns of regular steel, and they have the advantage of not migrating to other areas.

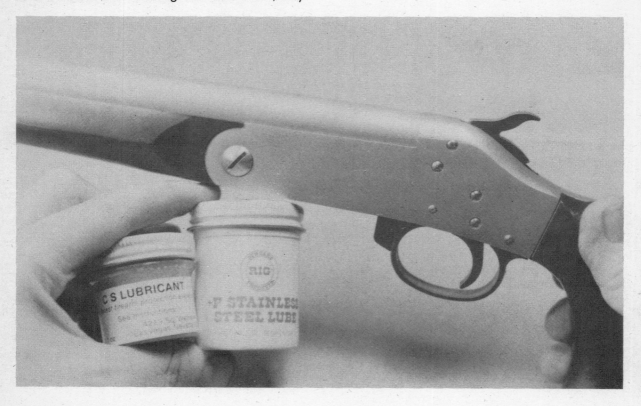

Muzzle-Loaders

I personally know only one man who regularly shoots a muzzleloading shotgun, but I know a large number who are blackpowder rifle shooters. Since the cleaning methods for both are identical, I'll just show rifles here. Because frequent thorough cleaning is so necessary with these guns, blackpowder rifles are made for easy total takedown. The old method of cleaning, with soap and plenty of hot water, will do a fine job of cleaning a muzzle-loader, but it's not the most convenient way. Also, the modern equipment and chemicals that are available will actually do it better. Here are my methods for cleaning blackpowder rifles:

1. Depending on the cleaning accessories used, the nipple of a caplock gun may or may not be taken off first, but at some point it will have to be removed and cleaned. Use a properly-fitted nipple wrench.

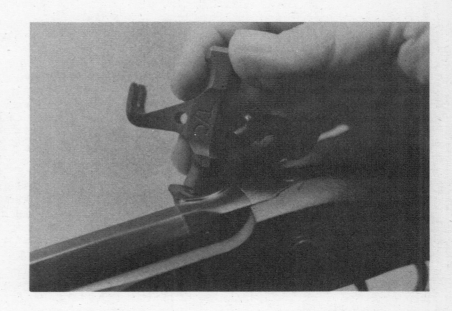

2. I often clean the nipple by inserting the applicator tube of a can of spray solvent, and blowing it out. Then, a pipecleaner is used to get any residue that was not dislodged by the stream of solvent. The bristle-type pipe-cleaners that were mentioned in the preceding shotgun section are also good here.

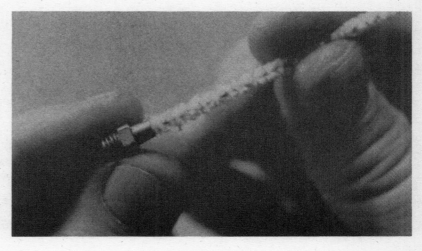

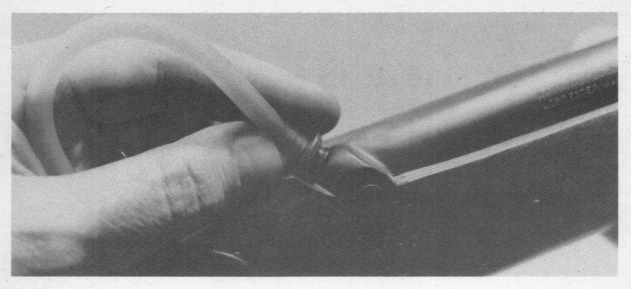

3. (Above) Uncle Mike's—Michaels of Oregon—has a kit called a Barrel Flusher that is a threaded fitting matched to the nipple threads in the drum and an ample length of rubber tubing. At the fitting, a rubber O-ring makes a tight seal when it is turned into place. Solvent is put into an open-topped container and the free end of the tube is dropped into it. A tight patch run back and forth in the bore creates a siphoning action. The cleaning solution is drawn into the bore, then expelled into the container. It's a neat system, and can be used without removing barrel from the stock.

4. (Below) Working on the same principle, the little bottle that comes with the Outers blackpowder cleaning kit does not require removal of the nipple. Its short tube of soft plastic just slips onto the nipple, and the solvent is put in the bottle before use. One advantage here is that smaller amounts of solvent can be used, and the bottle can be emptied and refilled with fresh solvent as it becomes fouled. In case you wondered, this neat little accessory is available from Outers separately, and is very inexpensive. Their catalogue number for it is 41520.

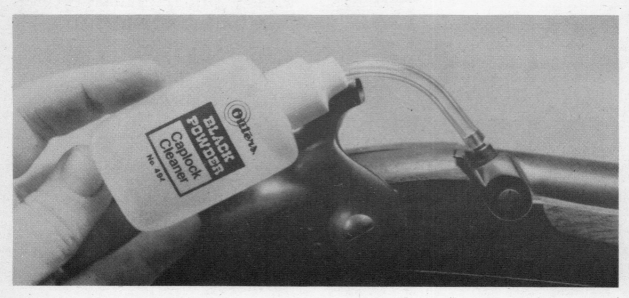

5. You can use regular bore brushes in muzzle-loaders, but it's a good idea to get brushes that are made especially for blackpowder use. They are exactly fitted to the bore, and they allow easy reversal at the end of the down-stroke. I usually do a brushing of the bore before going to the patch and solvent.

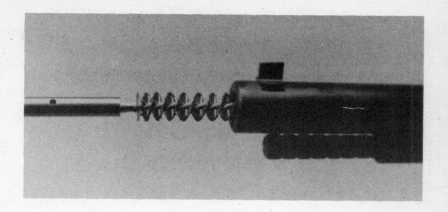

6. When you are not using the Michaels barrel-flusher unit or the Outers bottle, the first step is to plug the nipple, to prevent cleaning solvent from running out onto the stock. One neat way that I have used is to heat the end of a short piece of plastic aquarium tubing, pinch it shut, then slip it onto the nipple. Another easy way, shown here, is to insert the broken-off tip of a round toothpick in the nipple, and then gently let the hammer down on it, to hold it in place.

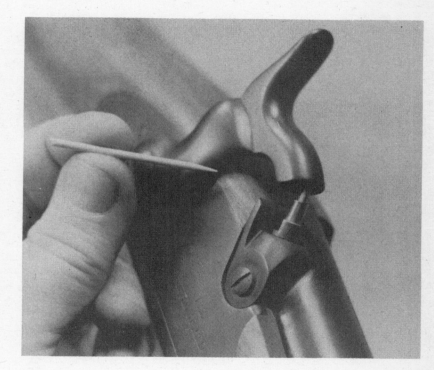

7. After the nipple is plugged, I apply solvent directly to the bore. If an aerosol can is used, about four short squirts is enough, in the average-length barrel. The amount can be varied, of course, according to the caliber and barrel length.

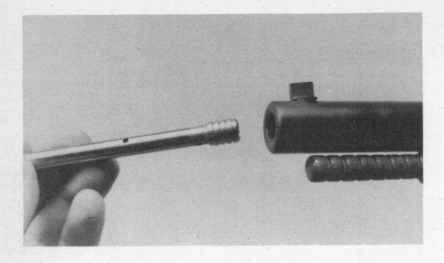

8. The jag tip used for black-powder cleaning must be carefully matched to the bore size and the thickness of the patch material. If it's too large, it can jam in the bore, and if it is undersize, the patch can slip off. When that happens, you'll need a "patch grabber" to get it out.

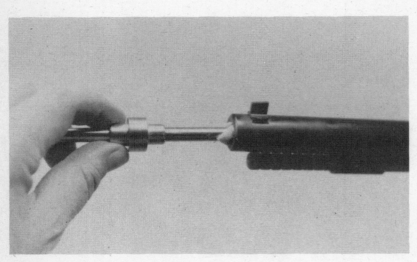

9. The patch can be pre-saturated by folding it double and tipping a solvent bottle, or, with a can of aerosol solvent, it can be started into the bore and the solvent applied at that point. If my method of direct application to the bore has been used, it won't be necessary to moisten the patch—it will pick up all it needs as it is run through the bore. Note the muzzle guard on the rod. After the patch is well into the bore, the knurled collar is used to hold the guard snugly in the muzzle.

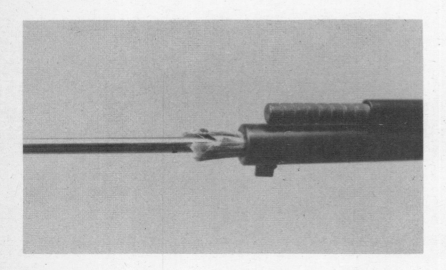

10. The first patch run will be heavily soiled, and can be discarded after two or three passes. As subsequent fresh patches are used, one will eventually come out clean, showing only the normal discoloration of the solvent. It should be noted that only a jag-type tip must be used, as a slotted tip would fail to get the patch to the rear wall of the chamber.

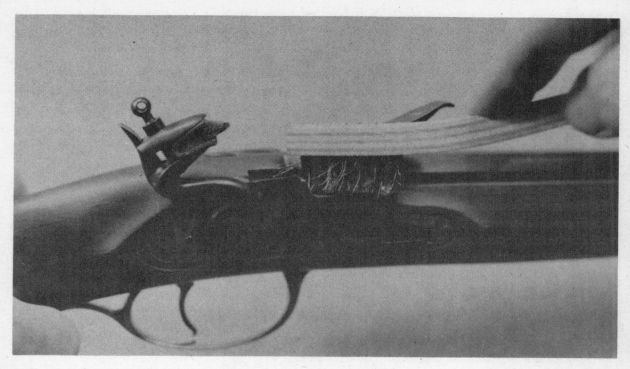

11. (Above) On a flintlock, the brush will do a good job of removing loose residue from the pan, but solvent should still be used on the area. Blackpowder film is very acid, and if it is not thoroughly removed, rust will quickly form.

12. (Below) When you're cleaning a flintlock bore, you can plug the touch-hole in the same way as noted for a caplock, but a longer piece of toothpick is used. The frizzen is lowered on it to hold it in place, and cleaning of the bore is done the same as in the caplock.

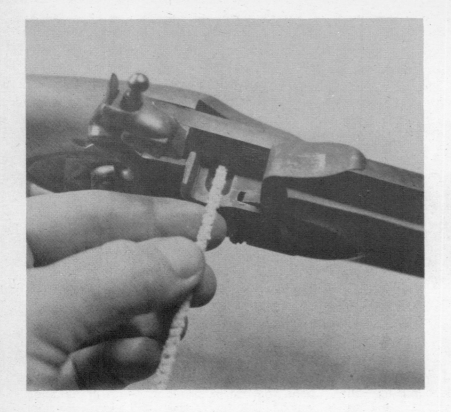

13. When the bore cleaning is completed, use a pipecleaner and some solvent to clear the touch-hole. The entire lock area should be scrubbed with solvent. In both flintlock and caplock, after extensive shooting, it's best to separate the lock, barrel, and stock for a thorough cleaning.

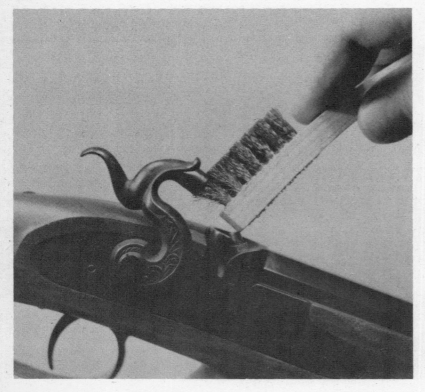

14. An area that is sometimes overlooked on caplock rifles is the interior of the hammer nose. Use a brush to clean out the residue that is left there by cap ignition and backflash from the nipple.

15. The backflash mentioned above, and the ignition flash from the cap, deposit a film on the lock area. Solvent and a brush or patch are used here.

16. (Right) Even with a jag tip of the proper size, you will occasionally lose a patch in the bore. This rod attachment, properly called a worm, will retrieve the patch. I've always called these things "patch grabbers." They are available from dealers in muzzle-loading supplies, in several forms.

17. (Below) When the cleaning is finished, the bore should be treated with a protectant. This can be done with a patch, but a mop attachment will do it better. When the gun is to be fired again, a dry patch should be run, to remove preservative from the bore. Also, a cap or two should be fired before loading, to clear out any protectant that might remain in the nipple. If these things aren't done, you may get a misfire.

18. (Left) In regard to oil on the internal mechanism, my advice is the same here as it was on the modern cartridge guns—just a little will do. Put a drop or two of oil on the hammer and sear engagement.

19. (Below) Put a drop of oil on pivots of the hammer and sear, and on hammer spring stirrup (or, if it's a coil mainspring, on the engagement of the spring plunger and hammer). A drop can also be applied where the sear spring (or spring plunger) meets the sear.

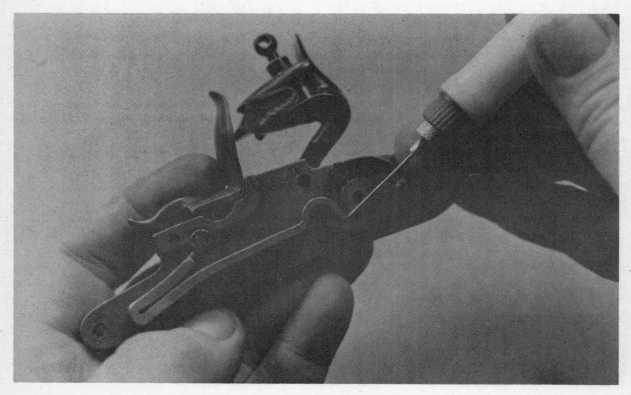

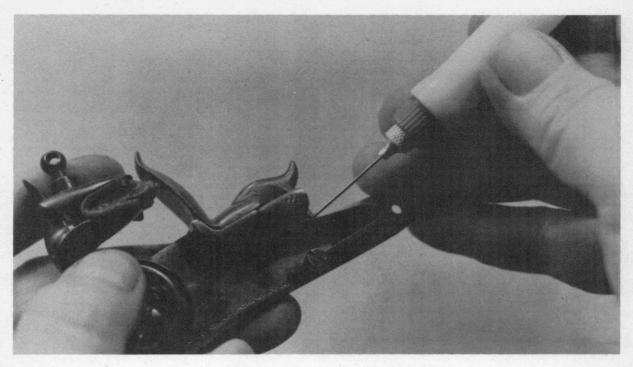

20. (Above) On a flintlock, in addition to the points noted above, there are two external locations that should get a drop of oil. One is the point of engagement of the lobe of the frizzen and the frizzen spring.

21. (Below) The other external flintlock location that should be oiled is the frizzen pivot.

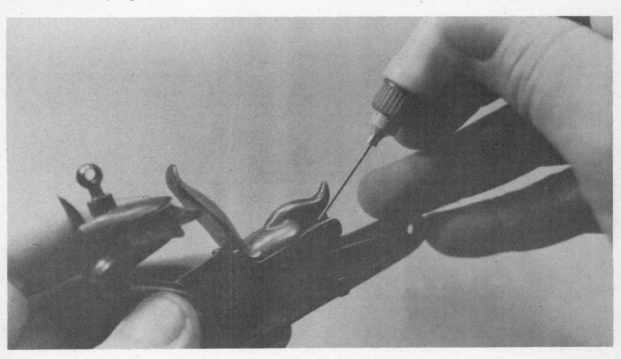

22. Treatment with a protectant can be done by direct spraying—if the protective solution is one that will not harm the stock finish. My method, as you know by now, is to put a small amount on the metal surfaces, and spread it by hand or with a cloth.

23. For longer storage, you can use RIG or Formula 15 Gunwax, or Rust Guardit. The last one mentioned is an aerosol wax in suspension, and it offers excellent protection without a sticky or greasy surface. It should be noted that brass, like the trigger guard of the Seneca rifle shown, also needs protection. It will fingerprint, and even if not touched it will have some surface changes over a period of time, just from atmospheric conditions.

A Final Note on Cleaning

As I noted back at the start of this part of the book, the cleaning methods described here are not supposed to be rules. They're just descriptions of the methods and equipment that I use, and they might have some value for the newcomer to the ranks of gun owners. A friend whose opinions I respect told me recently that those of us who write about firearms frequently make one mistake—we tend to assume that all of our readers are old experienced gun people, so we don't go into enough detail when we explain certain operations and features. Well, maybe this time I've included the simple details.

Section Three

Gun Refinishing

WHEN GUN OWNERS ask about refinishing, there are three questions that are always at the top of the list. They want to know when refinishing is necessary, and whether it will lower the value of the gun. The third question is not as easy to answer—which finish to choose. In this section of the book, I'll answer the first two, and then give detailed descriptions of the various finishes available, so the reader can decide for himself which one is best for his particular application of gun use.

Before we get into the real refinishing discussion however, there is one other question that comes up with some regularity: Can cold blue be used to give a good finish to an entire rifle or shotgun? For this one, there's an easy quick answer: No. As its name indicates, cold blue is a rapid-oxidizing agent in liquid or paste form that is useful for touch-up work. It can mask scratches, or color small parts, but it's not really

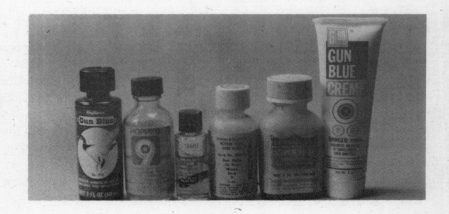

An assortment of cold blue solutions. They are fine for touch-up work, but are not suitable for doing a complete gun.

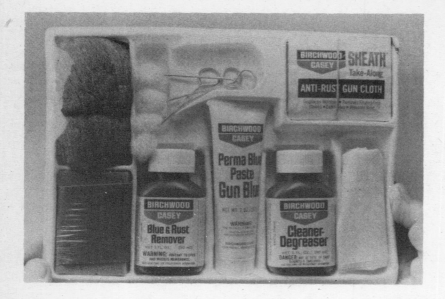

This cold blue kit from Birchwood Casey has all of the necessary items, and includes rust remover, a cleaner-degreaser, and Sheath protective cloth.

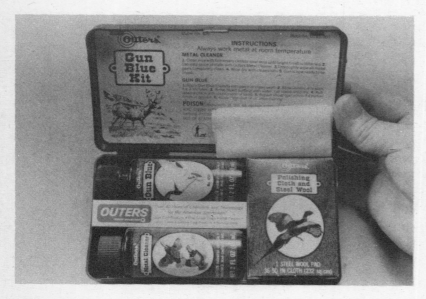

A simpler kit from Outers, containing only the essentials, but it will also do the job.

suitable for an entire gun. When all of the metal parts of a shotgun or rifle have been polished mirror-bright, and if cold blue is applied evenly and quickly, a fairly good finish can be imparted. However, there's a catch: It won't last. A cold blue finish doesn't have the depth that is given by the hot-bath process used by gunsmiths and manufacturers. With cold blue, the corner edges and high spots will start to show wear right away. Giving a high polish to all of the parts of a rifle or shotgun is the most demanding part of any refinishing process, so it's ridiculous to waste the effort expended on a mirror finish by using cold blue.

This is not to say, though, that cold blue doesn't have a number of good uses. I keep it on the workbench, and use it often. For example, a small scratch on an otherwise perfect blued finish can be hidden by dipping an ordinary round toothpick in cold blue, and rubbing it in the ex-

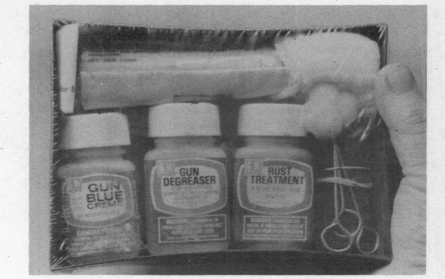

All of the cold blue kits are similar in content. This one is from Jet-Aer, with the G96 brand.

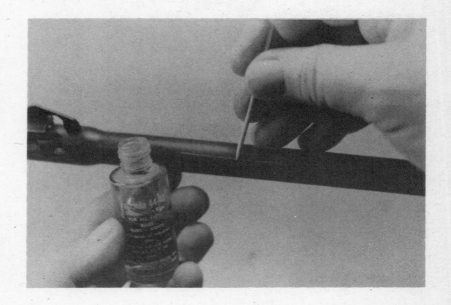

Scratches like the one shown are the particular province of cold blue. Here, a toothpick dipped in the solution is being used to apply blue precisely in the scratch.

Below—The same barrel is shown after application of cold blue. The scratch can still be located, but it is no longer bright and noticeable.

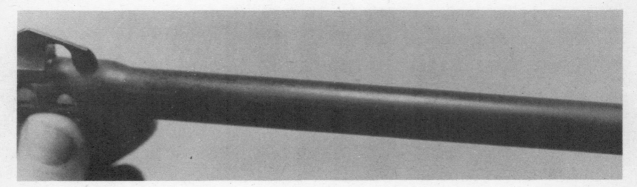

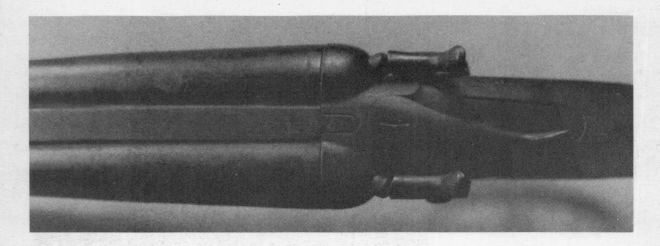

Above and left—A good candidate for refinishing, this old double shotgun has gone beyond wear to patches of surface rust.

While the metal parts are being refinished, some attention will have to be given to repairing several areas of the stock wood.

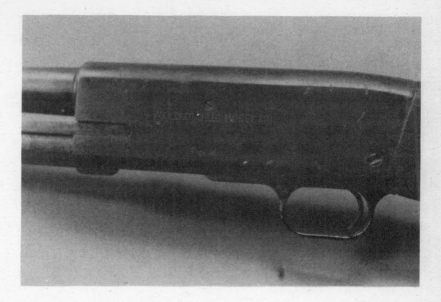

Another refinishing candidate. This old slide-action gun appears to have led a hard life.

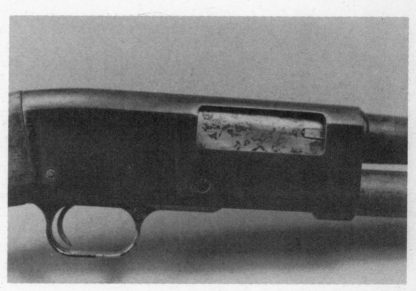

act line of the scratch. If you use this trick, don't allow a drop to cling to the toothpick—let the wood absorb the chemical, and that will be enough. Cold blue works best if the metal is warmed slightly. I leave items to be cold-blued under my 200-watt workbench light for a few minutes, and they're just right. One last note on cold blue: If there is a fairly large bare area on a nice blued finish, it is practically impossible to blend cold blue into the existing finish. This is

especially true if the original blue has a particularly deep lustre. The color and texture will hardly ever be a perfect match.

Now, let's get back to the first question, about when a rifle or shotgun should be considered for refinishing. We're talking now about guns for practical use, guns that have been made in large quantity, with no collector interest. (Those, we'll discuss later.) Any shotgun or rifle that sees a lot of use, for hunting, plinking,

Section Three: Refinishing

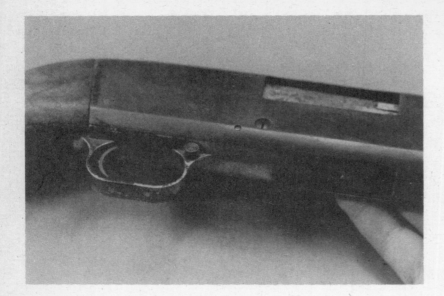

On the same gun, most of the anodizing has worn off the alloy trigger housing. It can be re-anodized, finished with Aluma-Hyde, or just polished bright.

or law enforcement, will inevitably have some wearing of the external finish. A blued finish will begin to show this earlier, but even some of the new finishes of other types are not immune to wear.

When wear occurs, it will first become evident on the corners and high areas, and also on parts that are subject to a lot of handling—bolt knobs, for example. Slide action and semi-auto shotguns will often show wear on the bottom of the receiver, just forward of the trigger guard. On most guns of this type, this is the balance point, and this is the place frequently cradled in the hand for carrying in the field. On guns with an exposed upper or lower tang at the stock wrist, the blue will soon thin there. Of course, the finish can be damaged by factors other than wear. For example, a lack of proper protection in humid climates can result in surface rust, and if this is left long enough, it can destroy the finish.

Whether from wear or damage, if there is bare steel showing in several places, refinishing should be considered. Even when it's kept covered with a protectant, bare steel has a tendency to rust. A light surface rust is easily removed by wiping with fine steel wool, and there may seem to be no real harm to the surface.

However, an examination under high magnification will show tiny pits in the steel. Under these conditions, a new finish is a matter of protecting the gun from further damage. Most often, gun owners will choose to have a finish that is the same as the original, but some may decide on a more durable alternative.

If the rifle or shotgun in question is a recently-made piece by a major manufacturer, factory refinishing may be considered. There are several advantages to this. The gun will be disassembled and reassembled by the same people who made it, and they may be more likely to see any problems that need to be corrected. If this is the case, factory parts are at hand. Also, if the gun is not in terribly bad shape, the finish can be virtually the same as when the gun was new. Not all manufacturers offer factory refinishing, so if you are thinking of this, it would be best to get in touch with the maker of your gun, and ask about the availability, the price, and shipping instructions. It should also be noted that refinishing usually takes longer at the factory than having it done at your local gun shop.

In having it done locally, the choice of a refinisher is even more critical than selecting a gunsmith for repair work. If a mechanical mistake is made, it can usually be corrected. A re-

The Stevens/Savage Model 73Y rifle mentioned in the text is shown before refinishing. Anodizing was chipped from the receiver and guard, and the steel parts had a patina of surface rust.

finishing mistake may not be reversible. The hot bath process, the chemical application of blue, is not a complicated operation—if the chemicals are fresh and the tank temperature is kept at the proper levels, the finish on the parts should be perfect. The factor that separates the expert from the amateur is the surface preparation of the steel. This precision polishing is an art. Unfortunately, not all practitioners are artists.

Even after the finish has been applied, it's easy to spot an inept polishing job. The edges of screw slots will be rounded, and the screw recesses in the receiver will be dished. Edges and corners of the major parts that are supposed to be sharp will be rounded off. On long straight lines or large flat areas, there will be waves. And, the markings on the gun, the factory name and other stampings, will be left faint, smeared, or even polished completely off. I was once told of a case in which an amateur refinisher, in his zeal to get every tiny pit polished away, removed the serial number from the receiver of a Winchester Model 12 shotgun. The owner of the gun was not amused. Neither, I imagine, was the BATF. Fortunately, the owner had a record of the original number, and it was re-stamped.

Gunsmiths and gun shops in my part of the country are very fortunate—we have the ser-

vices of Richard A. Floyd (5205 Sherbrooke Road, Evansville, Indiana 47710). For the professional gun people in this area, he has become *the* refinisher, and the rest of us have stopped doing it. We just do the disassembly and reassembly, and let Dick handle the actual refinishing. And, he is an artist. When he delivers the finished job, the markings are legible, the edges sharp, and the flat areas are flat. He can provide a matte or satin finish, or a high polish, or any combination of these. At the present time, he offers only blue finish and nickel plating. At one time, he also did a beautiful chrome, and I wish he still offered the finish, as it is a perfect match for polished alloy. He says, though, that chrome plating is a slightly more involved process, and at this time his backlog of work is so large that he can't take the extra time for it. The chrome mentioned above is the decorative type, and should not be confused with the hard chrome finishes such as Armoloy.

As noted in the preceding paragraph, the white "color" of chrome makes it a match with polished alloy, and I have used this feature in several refinishing jobs on guns having alloy trigger groups. The worn anodizing on the alloy part was polished off, and the trigger group left bare. The receiver was then done in satin

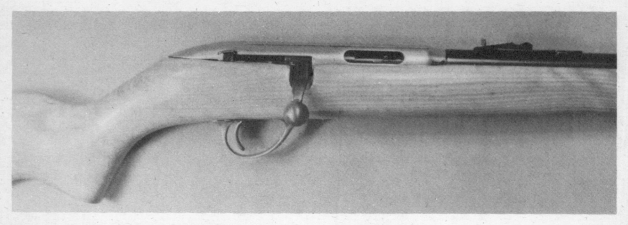

Above and below—The same gun shown on preceding page, after refinishing. The alloy receiver and guard were polished bright, and the barrel and other steel parts were reblued. The stock was done in natural color with Tru-Oil by Paul Fulkerson. The metal work was by Dick Floyd.

Left—On the same Model 73Y, the polished receiver and the deep blue of the barrel make a nice contrast.

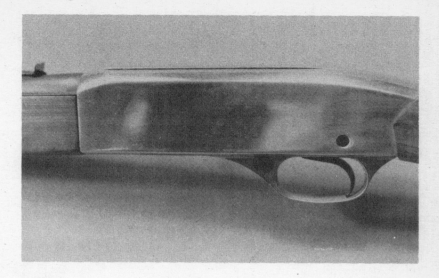

This Winchester Model 190 was given a similar treatment, and went from a very ordinary 22 rifle to the look of a custom gun. This gun was done several years ago, and the polished receiver is still bright.

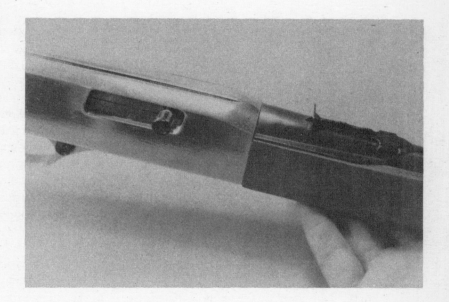

chrome, and the effect was as if the two parts had the same finish.

Even when there is no intention of matching the part with chrome, I often polish alloy and leave it bare. The black anodized finish on alloy can be re-done, but the expensive equipment to do it is usually not available locally, So, when I reblue a Remington Model 870 shotgun, for example, the trigger group is just polished and left bright. Similarly, I used this pattern on two 22

caliber rifles that are shown here. One is a Stevens (Savage) Model 73Y that I remodeled for my youngest son, shortening the stock and thinning the grip portion. The barrel and other parts were blued, and the receiver and guard, which were alloy, were just polished bright. Since he normally used a scope with this gun, the bright receiver top did not interfere with sighting. If it had, the top could have been done in matte finish. There is one thing to keep in mind when

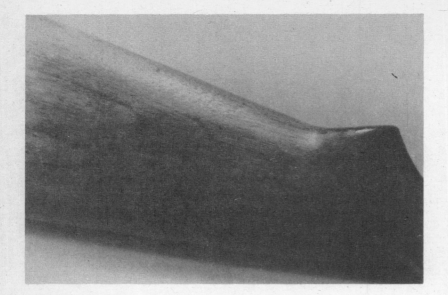

Here is a stock in dire need of refinishing. Along with numerous scratches and small dents, its surface had accumulated several patches of coating that were unidentifiable and unattractive.

polishing alloy in this manner: Dural and other mostly-aluminum alloys can be left bare and will retain their brightness and color for many years. Zinc-based alloys, though, will tend to acquire a grey color and some dullness with the passage of time.

The other 22 rifle that I did with this treatment was a Winchester Model 190 semi-auto. This rifle had been bought as a parts gun for the shop, and I later discovered that it needed very little repair to make it a working gun. After this was done, I decided to also restore its appearance. The barrel assembly and small parts were blued, and the badly worn anodizing was polished from the receiver and trigger group. The result, as you can see in the photos, was an attractive rifle. Although this was done several years ago, the surfaces of the trigger group and receiver are still bright.

Whether it's done on alloy or steel, the prefinish polishing controls the finished texture. To produce the matte or satin finish, the surface of the metal is air-blasted with fine sand or tiny glass beads. A different treatment, often seen on stainless steel guns, is the brushed finish, which is not as dull as matte, but less bright than a high polish. In the brushed finish, there will be tiny lines across the surface. The less-reflective textures are often used on the top of receivers, to prevent glare in the sighting plane. The use of matte finish is not restricted to the top, though— it is frequently used on the entire gun, especially on those which may be used in security or law enforcement work.

When a handgun is refinished, and the grips are badly damaged, they can simply be replaced. Actually, I've found that the grips on modern handguns are rarely in need of replacement or refinishing. This is not true, though, of rifles and shotguns. When the gun is worn and scratched, the stock wood will also show the same degree of long use. When this is the case, and the metal parts of the gun are refinished, the contrast will make the stock even worse. Most of the time, I recommend that the wood be done at the same time the rest of the gun is being refinished.

A stock can be done by simply sanding off the old finish and the worst of the scratches, hanging it up, and giving it a couple of coats of acrylic lacquer from a spray can. Unfortunately, this "quickie" method will be instantly recognizable to anyone who knows a good stock finish. And, the plastic surface, when it gets its first nick, will often start to peel off. My daughter's husband, Paul M. Fulkerson, does all of

When sanding a stock during the refinishing process, special care must be used in areas where the wood meets the metal parts of the gun. Any rounding of these edges will spoil the entire appearance, and may even cause later breakage.

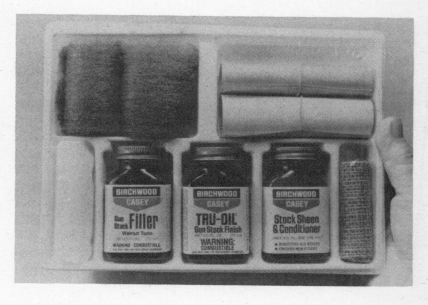

Since Birchwood Casey is the maker of Tru-Oil, it would be expected that their stock refinishing kit would be complete, and it is.

my stock work, and he uses Birchwood Casey Tru-Oil exclusively.

Just as polishing metal is an art, so is the sanding and smoothing of stock wood. Where the wood of the stock meets the metal of the receiver and other parts, this fit must be preserved. When an amateur sands a stock, he will usually round these edges, and the careful factory fitting is lost. Because of the soft nature of wood as a material, this is often harder to avoid

than when working with metal. It is especially difficult when the stock being refinished is old, and either oil-soaked at the edges, or dry and brittle.

After sanding with progessively finer paper, Paul uses ultra-fine steel wool to smooth the surface of the stock, then applies Tru-Oil. As many as six or seven complete coats may be used, with the surface hand-rubbed between the coats, as the grain is raised. When the final coat is

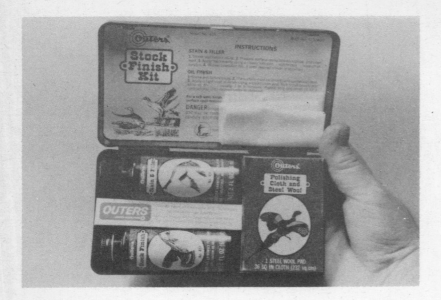

Less elaborate, but still containing the essentail elements, is this small stock finish kit from Outers.

Tru-Oil by Birchwood Casey comes in several forms and containers. The aerosol can is shown here, with the stock of the Savage/Stevens 73Y shown earlier.

applied, the stock is suspended in a dust-free environment to cure for a day or two, and then a wax is used. You will see the results in some of the photos here. This treatment brings out the natural beauty of the wood grain, a feature often hidden by factory ''walnut'' stain. Unless we are specifically told to do otherwise, we finish all stocks in their natural color, which is often lighter than their original finish. It complements a blued metal finish nicely.

For the careful amateur who wants to try it, there are several good stock-finishing kits available. Because Paul uses Tru-Oil, the first one that comes to mind is the kit by Birchwood Casey. It contains bottles of Tru-Oil, Filler, and Stock Sheen & Conditioner, along with sandpaper in two grades, fine steel wool, burlap and cloth, and instructions. Outers Stock Finishing Kit #455 is smaller, but contains all of the essentials. It includes Stain & Filler, Stock Finish,

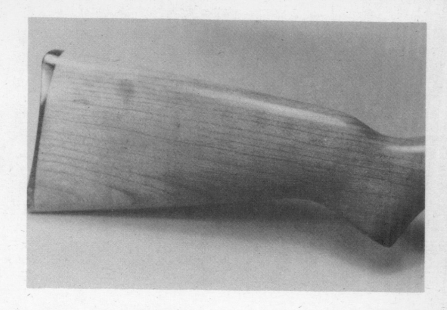

Here is the stock of the Winchester Model 190, finished in Tru-Oil. The finish shown was obtained with five separate coats, with the wood hand rubbed between each one.

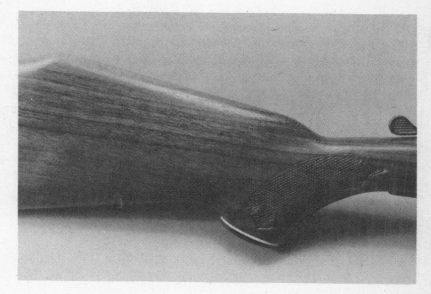

Another Tru-Oil finish. This stock had a particularly ugly surface stain, and it was hiding some nice grain. The impressed checkering was sanded very lightly.

sandpaper, steel wool, an applicator cloth, a polishing cloth, and instructions. With the proper care, either of these kits will produce a fine finish on any stock.

When a stock to be refinished has checkering on the grip area and the forend, and the checkering is badly worn, it is possible to re-cut it with a suitable tool, but this can be expensive. Most professional stock finishers charge for re-cutting checkering by the *line*. There's a good reason

for this. It requires a very steady hand and a good eye, and the checkering tool must be exactly matched to the dimensions of the original work. If the checkering is worn so thin that it's almost not there, it might make sense to just sand it off, and finish the area smooth, or have a new pattern cut.

Now, let's get back to the subject of refinishing the metal parts. Sometimes, routine refinishing of any type is absolutely not advisable. If

Section Three: Refinishing

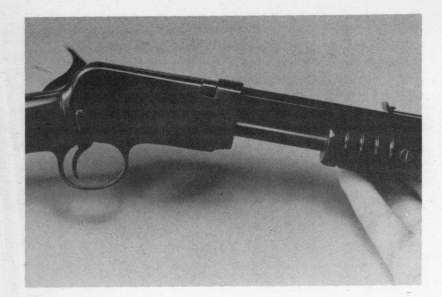

A simple job of fine rebluing, but also a perfect restoration. The Winchester Model 1890 shown was done as a gift for my father, James W. Wood. Note the cleanly-polished edges, especially the lines of the octagon barrel. The metal work was by Dick Floyd.

the shotgun or rifle in question is of interest to collectors, and has substantial value in that department, then it should not be given an ordinary reblue. I have seen some really terrible examples of this sort of thing. One was an 1873 Winchester rifle that had been buffed almost to death, then inexpertly reblued. All of its corners had been rounded, including the once-clean lines of its octagon barrel. The enthusiastic polisher hadn't quite managed to remove all of the markings on the barrel, though. You could still read, in flowing script, the words, "One of One Thousand."

Not quite as bad as this, but bad enough, was the case of the man who brought into a local gunshop for rebluing a gun that he called an old rifle. He wanted it made pretty, he said, to hang over the fireplace. He also wanted to know if he could get a reduced price on the reblue, since he had already taken off the rust. With an electic rotary wire brush, he had removed a hundred years of beautiful brown patina from an unconverted flintlock Model 1817 Harpers Ferry Artillery Musket. If a collector dreamed about an incident of this sort, he'd wake up in cold sweat. Unfortunately, this was a real occurrence. More than $1,000, flicked off by the steel bristles of that rotary brush.

Disasters of this sort are preventable, but only if gunsmiths and gun shop clerks know a collector piece when they see one. A while back, a man brought a fine old Parker Double to me for refinishing. It was well worn, with thin blue and faded color-casehardening. Internally, it was perfect. I suggested that it just be thoroughly cleaned and treated with a preservative, then put away. I also advised him to obtain a professional appraisal. He did, and even in its worn condition, the Parker was evaluated at more than $2,000.

If a gun is a valuable collector piece, and it is only slightly worn, with some original finish left, then it should not be refinished. Protect any thin areas from rust, and otherwise leave it alone. If the gun is extremely worn, with almost no finish and some pitting, then some consideration might be given to having it restored. This will entail far more than ordinary refinishing. It will call for special operations that will bring back the finish, as near as possible, to the appearance of the gun when it left the factory. For some guns, this can mean having a restoration specialist reblue by the old slow rust process, restore color-casehardening to certain parts, and so on. It's expensive, but it's often worth the price.

Guns that are intended primarily for police and other security use are often done entirely in matte finish, to prevent reflections. Shown is a Demro XF7 Wasp, a 9mm carbine.

Dick Floyd and I recently restored a fine old 12-gauge Remington Model 1889 double. It was mechanically tight, but all the finish was gone, and there were areas of surface rust. One firing pin retaining screw was rusted in place, and some previous attempt at removal had damaged its head. A new screw was made. Large quantities of ancient caked dirt and residue were removed from inside the receiver and the locks. Light polishing was done, to remove the small pits on the surface, but all factory markings were carefully preserved. The barrels and some of the small parts were blued by a special non-heat method. The receiver and locks were beautifully done in color-casehardening. The buttstock and forend were done in seven coats of Tru-Oil by Paul Fulkerson.

According to *Flayderman's Guide To Antique American Firearms* (available from DBI Books), the old Remington now looks almost exactly as it did when it was shipped out of New England at the turn of the century. And its owner, who had a $75 wall-hanger, now has a $400 collector piece. As noted earlier, this was a good, tight gun. There is a point at which restoration is not feasible—if the pitting is too deep, if major parts are missing, and so on. So, the points to be considered in deciding on restoration are the condition, and the collector value.

Collectors have divided opinions about restoration. One group believes that any gun that has been refinished, even though it may have had careful restoration, has almost no collector value. This group would rather have a gun with only traces of the original finish, in very worn condition, than one that has had professional restoration. The other groups says that as long as the work is done by an expert, with the result being as close as possible to the original factory finish, there is nothing wrong with restored pieces. Most of the time, I tend to agree with the latter group, but we're not going to settle this question here. Probably, not ever.

Let's get back for a moment to regular refinishing. In addition to the combination of matte and polished surfaces mentioned earlier, there are other attractive uses of contrast, and some of these have practical aspects. Manufacturers have used this principle in new guns, and it can be used for interesting variations in refinishing. In rifles that are otherwise totally blued, the bolts are often chromed or nickel plated. Quite a few rifles and shotguns have triggers that are gold-plated. Early Winchester rifles, and many of the other guns of that period, had receivers that were finished in color-casehardening, while the rest of the parts were blued. In all of these cases, the difference of the contrasting finishes is attractive, and it also offers advantages. The plating smooths the operation of the bolt, and if it's hard chrome, it wears better than bare steel. The gold trigger, often in contact with a fingertip, is immune to the acids in perspiration. And, the color-casehardening is *hard*, and resists scratches and rust.

Now, let's look at the finishes that are currently available, and detail some of their properties. Some are resistant to elements that will quickly affect other finishes, and some are more durable than others. In the estimation of the traditionalist, several of the finishes that are very wear-resistant and impervious to rust and corrosion are also unattractive. Recently, a visitor to my office, seeing a gun that has a new and very tough finish, commented that it looked like a toy. This particular gun, though, with its space-age finish, could be left out in the rain for a month, and it wouldn't rust. So, the choice of a finish, like so many other things, may be a compromise.

Brown

Today, browning is used mostly on modern blackpowder guns, and for restoring antiques. It differs from blue in surface texture and chemical composition, but like blue, it is a controlled rusting process. Even when the pre-polishing is bright, the surface of a browned gun will have a satin texture. Browning is unique, among the oxidized-surface treatments, in that it can be done well without a hot-bath process. The metal is warmed, the solution swabbed onto the sur-

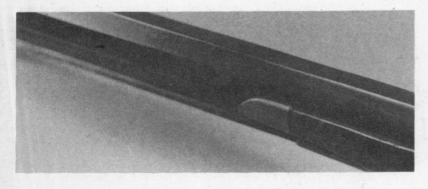

Two views of an expertly-re-browned barrel, showing the soft texture of this attractive antique finish. This caplock rifle was used by my great-grandfather in western Kentucky, before the Civil War.

Especially useful to those who build modern replicas of muzzle-loaders, this kit from Birchwood Casey has essentials for finishing both the metal and the wood.

Also designed for finishing all parts of a muzzle-loader is this kit from Connecticut Valley Arms.

face. This process is repeated many times for complete coverage.

Birchwood Casey has a fine browning solution called Plum Brown, and also offers a muzzle-loader's refinishing kit which includes stock finishing materials. Dixie Gun Works (Union City, Tennessee 38261) has an excellent browning solution, and Brownells offers Schrieber's, used by many professional blackpowder gunsmiths. Connecticut Valley Arms (5988 Peach-tree Corners East, Norcross, Georgia 30092) has a nice browning kit that also has essentials for Colonial-style finishing. My wife likes the browned finish, and she recently asked me why it isn't used on modern cartridge-type guns. There are two reasons, I think: The appearance would be a little odd, as if the gun had surface rust. And, blue and the other modern finishes are much more resistant to wear and damage.

Blue

There's no question that blue is the most popular and most economical finish for rifles and shotguns. Like brown, it is a controlled oxidation of the surface of the steel, and it can vary in color from a deep black to a very bluish light tone. Several factors govern the color—the type of steel to which it is applied, the chemical composition of the bluing salts, and the temperature of the bath. Sometimes a reddish tone is produced, and this can be the result of excessive bath temperature, or steel that is either heat-treated or of very low carbon content. The

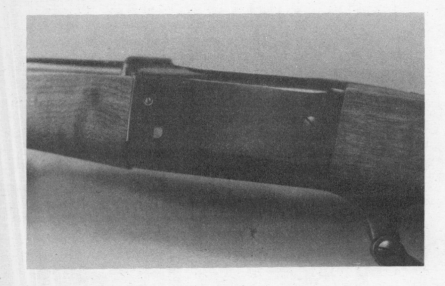

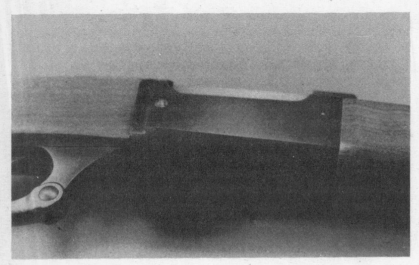

Original factory blue, as illustrated by this Savage Model 99A, has a luster that is difficult to match. Some manufacturers offer factory refinishing.

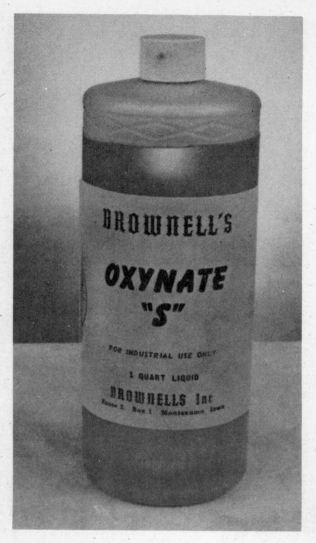

Oxynate S, available from Brownells, is used by professionals to avoid the reddish tinge that sometimes occurs with some steels.

For bluing by the old slow-rust method, Brownells offers Pilkington Rust Blue.

frames of some of the older low-priced single-barreled shotguns, for example, were practically cast iron. There is an additive called Oxynate S, available from Brownells, that can be added to the bluing bath to prevent the red color.

The hot bath method of bluing, using caustic salts, is the most widely used, but there are other ways. The old Belgian Method can be duplicated with Brownells Dicropan IM. this method uses hot water, no caustic salts, and it takes more time, but it will impart a fine finish. Another way is the old slow rust process, mentioned earlier in connection with restoration. As its name implies, it is also slow, but the results are worth the extra time. Pilkington Rust Blue solution for this method is available from Brownells.

Blue is always chosen by the firearms traditionalist as a finish for rifles and shotguns, and I'll admit that it does perfectly complement fine stock wood. In the eyes of many people, a gun just doesn't look like a gun unless the finish is blue. However, blue does have some disadvantages. It will wear off in time, especially in areas that are subjected to continuous rubbing, such as the points touching a rack in a car or truck. Any area that is in contact with perspiration or other moisture can rust—the previously mentioned carrying area forward of the trigger guard is an example. Treating with a protectant will retard this tendency, but it can't absolutely prevent it.

In choosing blue as a finish, it's better for target or sporting guns. These would normally have lighter use, better care, and less of a wear factor. If the gun is used for law enforcement, security, or personal defense, the heavier wear and exposure to the elements would indicate that a more positively protective finish should be chosen, such as Teflon-S or one of the other modern finishes. Now, of course, we are also beginning to see rifles and shotguns made entirely of stainless steel, and this really solves the problem.

Nickel

Plating with nickel is an electrolytic process, using a direct current. A bar of pure nickel is suspended from a non-conducting rod in an electrolytic solution, and connected to a positive terminal, or anode. The part to be plated is suspended on the other side of the tank, and connected to a negative terminal, or cathode. Applied current then causes the positive ions of nickel in the solution to be deposited on the part, and they are replaced in the solution by

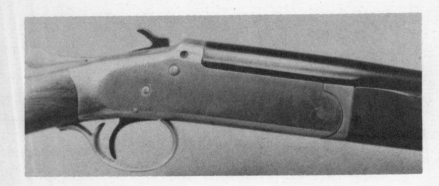

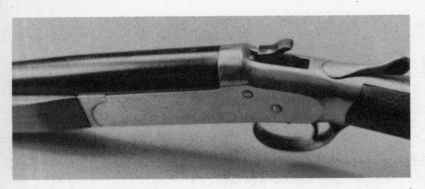

A combination of blue on the barrel, hammer, and trigger, and satin nickel on the other parts makes an old Iver Johnson Champion very attractive.

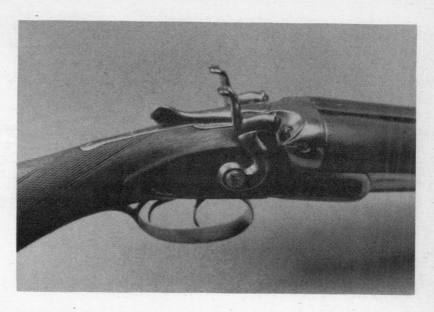

Another combination of blue and nickel, on an antique double shotgun.

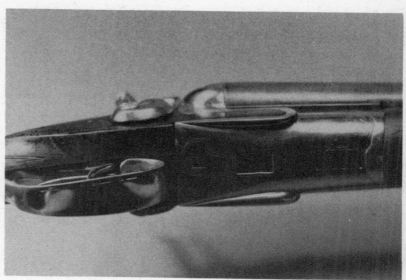

nickel from the bar. This process can be reversed, and it is used in that way to strip the old nickel from a part that is to be re-plated. The polishing and other preparation are much the same as for rebluing.

One advantage of nickel is that it is entirely rust-proof, and also resistant to most forms of corrosion. The surface of nickel will tend to discolor with age, and in certain atmospheric conditions. When this occurs, though, it can be re-polished to its original shine. If the surface is not broken, nickel is an excellent protective covering. It has more thickness and abrasion resistance than blue, so it wears well. It can be done in polished or matte style, and the latter is more often used today. Some aluminum alloy parts can be nickel plated, but other alloys sometimes can be damaged by the process, and can't be done.

For shotguns and rifles, nickel is rarely used

as a finish for the entire gun. Satin-finish nickel is used with some frequency on receivers, especially on shotguns. In earlier times, many single-barreled shotguns had receivers done in bright nickel. The bright polish, though, is seldom used now because of its light-reflective qualities. In law enforcement or self defense use, it could betray your location. In sporting use, it could interfere with sighting and startle game. Even with matte finish on top of the receiver, bright sunlight would make the sighting plane less clear.

There is another disadvantage of nickel that develops with wear and age. When a sharp edge is worn, the nickel can start to peel, and exposed areas of bare steel will then be likely to rust. It should be noted that when this occurs, the rust will not necessarily be confined to the exposed area—it can extend in all directions from that spot, under the plating. For this reason, when a nickeled receiver or other part shows signs of peeling, it should be re-nickeled right away, before pitting occurs.

In recent times, my only use of nickel has been in the restoration of old guns that had it as an original finish, and for plating certain parts that received a lot of wear, such as triggers and safety buttons. It has some value in these uses, but not as an over-all finish. And, it has been superceded by several finishes that are less reflective and more durable.

Chrome

As a metallic substance, chrome was discovered nearly 200 years ago, in 1797. Until the late 19th century, it was considered by metallurgists to be no more than a laboratory curiosity. The old methods of extracting it from chromium ore made it difficult and expensive to obtain, because of its high resistance to heat and chemicals. Around 1915, new extraction methods were developed, and chrome became a valuable additive for steel alloys. It also began to be used as a protective plating on many items, including firearms. As a protective finish, chrome plating

Satin chrome was used here on a single part, the barrel latch.

is superior to nickel in several ways. The surface is harder, and more resistant to scratches and other damage. Chrome resists chemicals that can affect nickel, and it does not tarnish in some atmospheres as nickel does. Its hard surface seems to wear forever, so it is less likely to peel and expose bare spots, even with tough usage. Its color is whiter than nickel, and as has already been noted, it matches well with polished alloy.

Since it is relatively more difficult to apply than nickel, its use as a firearms finish has been somewhat limited. Today, its most often seen application is in a satin texture, on the receivers of better-quality over/under shotguns, and on some doubles. When Dick Floyd was still doing chrome plating, I used it many times for just that purpose. I remember one instance, involving a beautiful and massive 10-gauge Spanish AyA Matador double that was owned by an avid goose-hunter. Every year, at the end of the season, he brought in this gun for refinishing, and its blued finish was marred with patches of surface rust. He apparently gave it hard usage in bad weather, and usually carried it by gripping the receiver, just forward of the guard. The next time it was brought in, we did the receiver and all other parts, except the barrels, in satin chrome. The appearance of the gun was greatly enhanced, and in subsequent years, only the barrels had to be refinished.

Among the current makers of doubles and over/unders, the choice of receiver finishes seems to be about equally divided between satin chrome and color-casehardening. The latter does offer more protection than blue, and it has an attractive appearance, but the chrome has superior protective qualities. Also, in the satin finish, it is not overly light-reflective. Like nickel, chrome can peel if its surface integrity is broken, but it is less likely to do this because of its hardness and resistance to wear.

Black Chrome

As far as I know, black chrome was offered by only one firm, the Marker Machine Company of Charleston, Illinois. It may be that they are still in business, but they have not offered black chrome as a firearms finish for more than 10 years, and no one else has offered it since. Black chrome is a mixture of regular chrome and a black oxide, in a proportion known only to Mr. Marker. At one time, it was a popular means of applying a dark finish to stainless steel parts. Now, of course, this can be done in several other ways.

During the time it was available, I had the black chrome finish applied to several handguns, but never had an occasion to use it on rifles or shotguns. It was available in two styles, matte and high polish. The matte was an even grey, and resembled a smooth Parkerizing. The bright finish was very attractive, a deep black that was reminiscent of old English charcoal blue. Both types, because of the oxide in the mixture, were not as hard as regular chrome, and they were more susceptible to wear and scratches. Still, it was a coating with chrome content, and it gave better protection than blue.

Silver and Gold

As a total finish, the precious metals are not normally used on rifles and shotguns. I have never seen a long gun that was entirely gold or silver plated, but these high-value metals are frequently used as embellishments on commemorative and presentation pieces. In earlier times, they were even used occasionally in a small way on otherwise unremarkable shotguns and rifles, especially those made in Europe. It is not at all unusual to come across a no-name Belgian double with the words "Fine Twist" inlaid in the top rib—in gold.

Today, gold and silver are mostly used to fill engraved lines or to highlight figures on elaborately-decorated guns. Browning and Marlin have also used gold on the triggers of shotguns and rifles. In practical use, silver will tarnish unless it is frequently polished, and gold is soft and wears quickly. Finally, for the average gun owner, the cost of these metals would rule them out for any serious consideraton as a firearms finish.

Except for ornate presentation pieces, precious metals are rarely used in firearms finishes. There has been one part frequently gold-plated, though, as shown by the triggers of this double shotgun.

A nice touch used by some refinishers is application of a bright filler in the markings of the gun. Here, silver Lacquer-Stik is used.

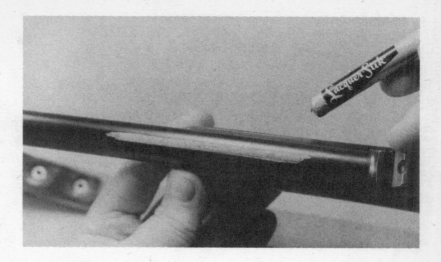

When the excess is wiped away, the markings stand out in silver. Lacquer-Stik, avaliable from Brownells, also comes in white and gold, and in red and black for use on lighter finishes.

Another way of filling the lettering is with a Bonanza Silver or Bonanza Gold kit, also offered by Brownells.

Parkerizing

While this is often used as a generic term for any phosphate-type finish, true Parkerizing was developed by the Parker Company of Detroit, Michigan, around 1925. Actually, there are several different phosphate finishes, and each has a slightly different texture and color. Over the years, U.S. Ordnance has used three principal types on our military arms. Zinc phosphate, a finish that was used on many World War Two guns, has a light grey tone. Duracoat, a phosphate coating over zinc plating, imparts a greenish (olive drab) appearance. Both of these were phased out in military use some years ago. Manganese iron, a process still used, is the most wear-resistant, and it gives a dark grey to black finish.

When these finishes are used commercially, they are also known by different trade names. The Parker Company calls the manganese iron process Lubrite #2, and the Heatbath Corpora-

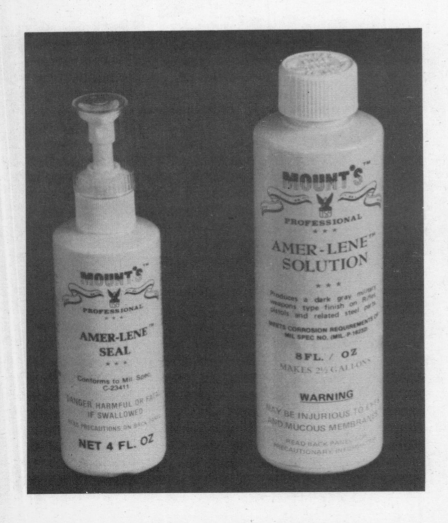

For those who want to try military-style phosphating at home, Brownells has Amer-Lene. It comes as a kit, as shown, with the concentrated solution and a sealer.

tion of Springfield, Massachusetts, uses the designation M-22 for the same process. By whatever name, the application of phosphate finish is similar to bluing. Special tanks of 300-series stainless steel are used, and the temperature range is more critical. The even heat of electric coils is preferred. It is a U.S. Ordnance requirement that the surfaces be grit-blasted with fine silica sand before phosphating.

Several years ago, I had a military gun re-phosphated by the manganese iron process. The finish was an even dark grey, and the smallest of the rust-pits that were present were entirely eliminated during the pre-treatment sand-blasting. I still have this gun, and shoot it occasionally. The finish has held up well. It was done by a firm that is no longer in business, and the only company now in my file that offers phosphating of firearms is Electrofilm, Incorporated, 22727 Avenue Scott, Valencia, California 91355. For those who may want to try it, Brownells has Amer-Lene, which will give a nice grey phosphate finish when properly used.

Color-Casehardening

The casehardening of steel is a heat-and-quench operation that is a form of surface tempering. The part is slow-heated to a certain temperature which is maintained for a specified period, and then is plunged into water or some other liquid, depending on the steel type. This imparts a very hard surface, but it won't produce the "oil slick" color, the attractive mottling, that is characteristic of color-casehardening. This can be achieved in several ways, all involving the use of chemicals in conjunction with the heat-and-quench operation. In earlier times, some of the chemicals used for this purpose were poisonous.

The method Dick Floyd uses to produce his beautiful color-casehardening effects is his own secret. I've managed to get a similar cosmetic effect by swabbing the surface with cold blue in a random pattern before applying heat. I will note here that the "straw" coloring of small

Color-casehardening is still occasionally used as a surface finish, as demonstrated by the receiver of a Savage 24D.

Action lever of a Savage Model 99A demonstrates the attractive mottling characteristic of color-casehardening.

parts is also a heat-and-quench operation, but without any chemicals being used. In the restoration of antique arms, both of these processes are frequently used.

Anodizing

Aluminum alloy and other non-ferrous alloys are color-coated in a process known as anodizing. It's similar to electroplating, but with different materials. Most of the anodizing used on firearms is a black or blue-black color, to match the blued finish on the steel. In resistance to wear, anodizing is about the same as nickel plating. It's more susceptible to scratches and other damage, though, because of the softness of the alloy that it covers.

The most common use of anodizing on rifles and shotguns is on trigger gurards and trigger groups made of alloy, but some 22 caliber rifles have entire receivers of this finish. When anodizing is scratched, or is thinned by wear, you can mask very small bright spots by using a felt-tipped marker that has permanent ink. I have seen attempts by owners to refinish scratched anodizing by using black spray-enamel, but the regular hardware-store type does not adhere properly to the alloy, and flakes off rather quickly.

Brownells has an alloy-refinishing kit called Aluma-Hyde that is the next best thing to genuine re-anodizing. It includes a zinc-chlorate primer and a special nitro-cellulose lacquer. They make no claim that it is as good as anodizing, but it does a good job and wears well. If you want genuine anodizing, you'll find that there are few facilities that will do it on a single-piece basis. One that does is Techplate Engineering, 1571-H South Sunkist, Anaheim, California 92806. The cost is comparable to having a similar part blued, plus shipping, of course.

If none of the above is feasible for one reason or another, there is always the alternative mentioned earlier: Just polish the part and leave its surface bare. If it is aluminum alloy, it will stay bright for years, and any new scratches can easily be polished away. Even if the alloy is zinc-based, and it turns grey, it will still look a lot better than a scratched or worn black finish. Whenever I refinish a gun that has alloy parts, I always just polish them, unless the customer specifically asks for re-anodizing.

Teflon-S

In the first years after its development, Teflon was used mostly on household utensils—steam irons, skillets, and so on. Then, some bright person realized that this space-age coating would make a great protective finish for firearms. Before we go any further, let's note that Teflon is a registered trademark of the DuPont Company. In firearms applications, a principal

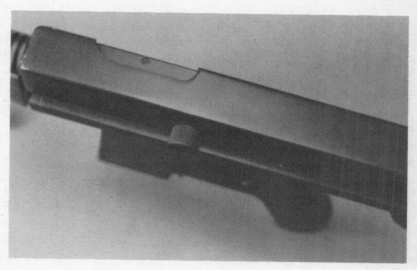

A Commando Carbine is shown before (above) and after (below) the application of Teflon-S. The expert work was done by Ronnie Butler of SECOA.

purveyor is West Coast SECOA, 3915 Highway 98 South, Lakeland, Florida 33801. Teflon has had several improvements since its beginning, and these have added designations, such as Teflon II. The one presently used by SECOA is called Teflon-S.

This is not the same as the Teflon that is used on kitchen items. It is an industrial type that is cured at 650 degrees Fahrenheit to form three layers, with the innermost layer forming a chemical bond with the metal surface. Except for the springs and the bore, all of the parts of a gun can be coated, whether they are steel or alloy. Teflon-S has a very low friction coefficient, so the action is smoothed. It is self-lubricating,

non-reflective, and sheds water and powder residues. Salt water, fingerprints, perspiration, and most solvents have no effect on its surface. When it is applied by a DuPont-licensed firm like SECOA, it is extremely durable.

One disadvantage of Teflon-S is that it can be scratched by contact with a sharp object. But then, that's true of many other finishes. Even so, it is not soft, and it will last a long time with reasonable care. Because of its high resistance to water and corrosives, it is a perfect choice for guns that are kept or used on boats. It is also popular, I'm told, with law enforcement people in coastal locations, where the guns used are in constant exposure to salt air.

Armoloy and Other Hard Chromes

The first of several hard chrome applications to firearms, Armoloy is even harder than most industrial chromes. It has a Rockwell C number of about 70, and this means that it's harder than many files. It would be an understatement to describe this finish as durable. It is, of course, impervious to corrosion and rust, and will even survive temperatures up to 1300 degrees Fahrenheit. It's possible that an Armoloy-surfaced gun might even survive a fire, and need only replacement of the stock and the springs. The application, though, is a low-temperature process—only 136 degrees.

The thickness of Armoloy is only two ten-thousandths of an inch, so there is no problem with reassembly after application, as is sometimes the case with other types of plating. The appearance is attractive, a matte-texture silver-grey, and it is actually less reflective than a high-polish blue. One other advantage of Armoloy is a measurable reduction in friction. At the engagement point of two steel parts, the fric-

tion coefficient is 0.20. When the two surfaces are coated in Armoloy, the figure reduces to 0.12. For more information, the address is: The Armoloy Company, 204 East Daggett Street, Fort Worth, Texas 76104.

There are other hard chrome finishes that have identical properties, including the degree of hardness and all of the other advantages. There are slight differences in color, but all are shades of silver-grey. One of the other hard chrome finishes that I have used is Metaloy. It is a darker grey than Armoloy, and seems to have a different surface texture. I realize, of course, that the texture is partially determined by the pre-finish polishing, but even allowing for this, the Metaloy surface seems slicker. It's a beautiful finish. The address is: Metaloy Industries, Incorporated, Route 3, Box 211-D, Berryville, Arkansas 72616.

Another of the hard chrome finishes that I have seen, but have not actually tried, is Metalife (Box 53, Reno Industrial Park, Reno, Penn-

Above and below—Two examples of beautiful Metaloy, a hard-chrome finish. Jim Kelley of Metaloy supplied these photos.

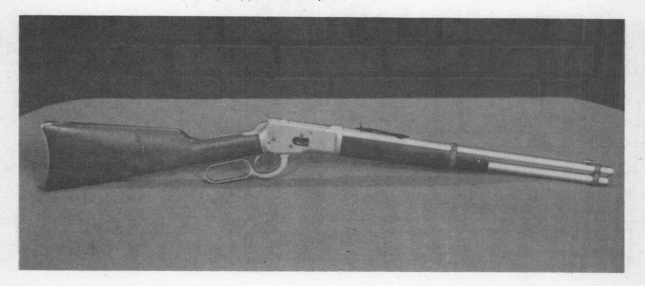

sylvania 16343). All of these hard chrome finishes are resistant to scratches, but if they are scraped with an object that is sharp enough and hard enough, their matte surface can be marked. If this happens, it will be just that, a bright mark, with the actual surface unbroken.

Electroless Nickel

Discovered around 1945, electroless nickel is a nickel alloy surfacing that is applied without the use of an electric current. In recent years, it has had quite a lot of use on firearms. There are several advantages over regular nickel plating, and perhaps the most important of these is the fact that electroless nickel gives a uniform thickness of plating over the entire part. In the regular nickel process, the edges of the item are given the heaviest deposit of nickel, the flat

critical. Electroless nickel can be applied to regular steel, stainless steel, nickel alloys, beryllium copper, sintered metals, and aluminum alloys. The process will damage zinc alloys, so it can't be used on them. The Rockwell C range is 49 to 53, and it can survive bending to 180 degrees without cracking or peeling. Parts coated in electroless nickel have been tested for more than 96 hours in direct salt spray without rusting. In appearance, it can be either satin or high-

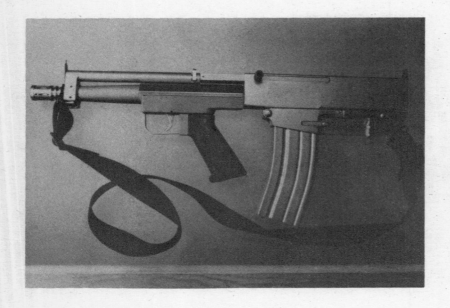

A factory application of electroless nickel, offered as an optional finish by Bushmaster. This is matte-style.

surfaces get a thinner plating, and the recesses get very little, or none at all. Also, the chemicals used in regular plating are usually metallic cyanide salts, and there are shipping problems. Mild acids are used in the electroless nickel process, but these can be easily shipped, or can be purchased locally.

Heat bath tanks and mild agitation are used in the application of electroless nickel, and keeping the temperatures within a certain range is

polish, or a combination of the two. Since it's a special alloy, it is whiter than regular nickel, and it can be finished to look a lot like stainless steel.

Brownells (Route Two, Box One, Montezuma, Iowa 50171) has all of the equipment for electroless nickel in their catalogue. Famed gunsmith Ralph Walker wrote the instructions for Brownells, and I'd like to quote him here: "The equipment needed is minimal—a couple of plastic pans, an old sink, a heat source, a couple of Grandma's Blue-Rock canners, and a stirring mechanism. Plus, the patience and intelligence to read and follow the instructions, particularly the cleaning instructions, to the letter.'' It's an excellent finish, and it's being used by several manufacturers on new guns.

Perhaps the best-known commercial application of electroless nickel is Nitex, and Ed House and his people do a fine job. Four years

ago, at the SHOT Show in New Orleans, I examined a gun that appeared to be made of stainless steel. However, at that time, this particular gun was not offered in stainless steel. It was, of course, finished in Nitex. As previously noted, electroless nickel can be made to look very much like stainless. The address for Nitex is: 2910 Belmeade, Carrollton, Texas 75006. If you want to call for more information, the number is 214–446–1197.

Looking a lot like stainless steel, this is Nitex, a professional application of electroless nickel. The photo is courtesy of Ed House.

Lubri-Bond

This is both a finish and a lubricant, and it's a process offered by Electrofilm, Incorporated, 27727 Avenue Scott, Valencia, California 91355. Lubri-Bond is molybdenum disulfide in a resin base, and in some applications it can reduce the coefficient or friction between mating parts to as little as 0.02. Before the application of Lubri-Bond, the steel surface should be sandblasted or glass-beaded, and for a superior bond, it should also be Parkerized. When the

finish is applied by Electrofilm, a Type M military phosphate is used before the Lubri-Bond is applied. Lubri-Bond is cured either by air-drying for 18 to 24 hours, or in an oven at 300 degrees for 1 hour.

With the air-drying option, it's possible to do even the springs, along with all the other internal parts. The finish has a light grey color and a smooth matte surface. Lubri-Bond can be scratched, and there will also be bright silver

marks at the engagement of parts, but this does not mean that the surface of the finish is broken. When compressed, molybdenum disulfide has a silver color, and its lubricating qualities are not affected by this. Since the finish itself is a high-grade lubricant, there's actually no need to use any oil in the mechanism. I recently assembled a gun done by Electrofilm in Lubri-Bond, and without any added lubricants, the action was unbelievably smooth.

The same idea can be applied to the outside. There is no need for the addition of any protectants, because Lubri-Bond meets or exceeds the military specifications for corrosion-resistance. It will take 240 hours of salt-fog exposure without a sign of rust. This is the same as an immersion in salt water for 240 days! Lubri-Bond is dry to the touch, and dirt, sand, and powder residue will not stick to its surface. It can be applied to aluminum or zinc alloys. It can also be used on stainless steel, and will not only impart a dark, non-reflective finish, but will also prevent galling, an occasional problem with some guns made of this material.

In addition to offering factory-applied Lubri-Bond, the Electrofilm company also has a kit that allows anyone to treat his gun with Lubri-Bond. It has two 3-ounce aerosol containers, one a de-greaser, and the other Lubri-Bond. It sells for about $10. When the finish is applied by the factory, including the pre-application Parkerizing, the cost is about the same as the average reblue.

Lubri-Bond by Electrofilm, Incorporated, is an even grey finish that is its own lubricant. In factory application, the guns are Parkerized before the Lubri-Bond surface treatment. Photo supplied by Frank Droege.

Kolene QPQ

The acronym above is a registered trademark of Kolene Corporation (12890 Westwood, Detroit, Michigan 48223), and the letters stand for Quench-Polish-Quench, a reference to the sequence used in the application of this finish. Kolene QPQ can be used as an excellent corrosion-resistant finish for regular steel, and it will surpass the qualities of both hard chrome and electroless nickel. One of its most interesting qualities, though, is that it can be used to impart a

little pistol was taken out of the box, new. The Fraser is made of stainless steel, so it doesn't need the superb protection of QPQ. If it did, though, this is one tough finish.

The process that makes it is a salt-bath liquid-nitriding, followed by mechanical polishing, and then a final immersion in a quench bath. From this sequence, a unique metallurgical surface is created. The oxygen-rich iron nitride on the surface has wear resistance and corrosion re-

Just as with several preceding photos, there was no rifle or shotgun available to show this finish. So far, it is available only on the Fraser 25 Auto. It's the QPQ finish, by Kolene Corporation. Under the smooth black surface, the little gun is stainless steel.

deep, black, and durable finish to stainless steel.

So far, my only encounter with the Kolene QPQ finish has been its use as a factory option on the Fraser 25 automatic pistol. My own Fraser with the QPQ black finish has been carried for about 7 months, and fired with some frequency. The finish still looks as it did when the

sistance properties that make it tougher than chrome or nickel. At the time this is written, the QPQ finish is available only on the Fraser pistol. However, the Kolene Corporation is licensing the process to commercial heat-treating companies, and perhaps one of them will offer it as a firearms finish. I hope so.

SS Satin Black

Another black finish for stainless steel is offered by Clinton River Gun Service (30016 South River Road, Mount Clemens, Michigan 48045), and it's called SS Satin Black. I have seen it only in photos so far, but it appears to be a deep and attractive finish. According to Darrell Reed of Clinton River Gun Service, it is a hot-bath process, and it does not involve electroplating. Those who want more information can write to the address above, or call 313–468–1090.

A Final Note on Refinishing

There are one or two finishes that I intentionally did not cover in detail here, as there seems little chance they will be used as replacement finishes. Before World War II, the military firearms of France had a black baked-on enamel finish that was remarkably durable. In more recent times, the Austrian Steyr GB pistol has a frame with a black crackle finish that seems to be very resistant to wear or damage.

There are three main factors to be considered in the selection of a finish: Protection, Appearance, and Light Reflection, in no particular order. One of these points will have more importance than the others, and the finish can be chosen on that basis.

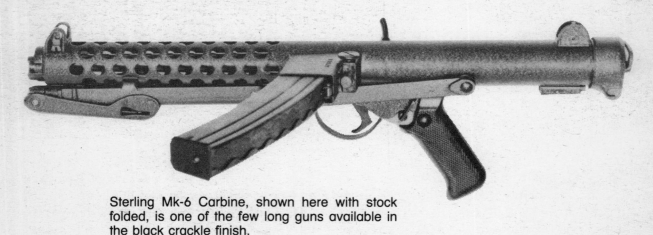

Sterling Mk-6 Carbine, shown here with stock folded, is one of the few long guns available in the black crackle finish.